Praise for
Before You Were Mine

Throughout the Bible, it is often *story* that gives both individuals and entire communities their sense of their identity and purpose, and God's work in history for their good. Helping our children see and interpret the unmatched story that God has given to them is a sacred role that carries life-long consequence. *Before You Were Mine* helps parents give this gift to their adopted children in a way that will guide and nurture them for a lifetime.

— Jedd Medefind, President,
Christian Alliance for Orphans

This book is a practical resource for cherishing and remembering your child's unique story, pre- and post-adoption.

— Ted Kluck, author of
Hello, I Love You: Adventures in Adoptive Fatherhood

Truly loving the hearts of relinquished and adopted children means respecting their birth parents, honoring their birth stories, and tracing the movement of God's hand in their pre-adoption lives. *Before You Were Mine* is a treasure for adoptive families, a chest filled with wise and healthy ideas and attitudes towards the relinquished child's story of loss, no matter what the reason may be. Adoptive parents who hope to "do right" by their children will find this text helpful in plotting the trail of adoptive development as it lays out in useful detail the steps that may be taken to bring forward these tender stories of early love and loss in life. TeBos and Woodwyk have their hearts and their book in the right place!

— Rev. Ron Nydam, PhD
Author of *Adoptees Come of Age*

TeBos and Woodwyk are inspirational, informative, challenging, and sincere in this honest discussion about the intricacies and tensions involved in the adoption story. It is clear that God will use this book over and again to help adopted people heal more fully from the wounds of relinquishment.

— David Thornsen, PsyD
Fountain Hill Center

This book gives a deeper and fuller understanding of the unique and special story of every person who is adopted. For parents and family members of adopted children, this journey is worth taking.

— Kristen Bell, MA OT
Founding Member of Mars Hill Bible Church

Before You Were Mine

Before You Were Mine

DISCOVERING YOUR ADOPTED CHILD'S LIFESTORY

SUSAN A. TeBos · CARISSA R. WOODWYK

FOREWORD BY SHERRIE ELDRIDGE

ZONDERVAN®

ZONDERVAN.com/
AUTHORTRACKER
follow your favorite authors

ZONDERVAN

Before You Were Mine
Copyright © 2007, 2011 by Susan A. TeBos and Carissa R. Woodwyk

This title is also available as a Zondervan ebook.
Visit www.zondervan.com/ebooks.

This title is also available in a Zondervan audio edition.
Visit www.zondervan.fm.

Requests for information should be addressed to:

Zondervan, *Grand Rapids, Michigan 49530*

Library of Congress Cataloging-in-Publication Data

TeBos, Susan A.
    Before you were mine : discovering your adopted child's lifestory / Susan A. TeBos and
Carissa R. Woodwyk ; foreword by Sherrie Eldridge.
        p.   cm.
    Includes bibliographical references (p. 167).
    ISBN 978-0-310-33103-2 (softcover)
    1. Adopted children — Biography — Handbooks, manuals, etc. 2. Scrapbooks — Handbooks,
manuals, etc. 3. Adoption — Religious aspects — Christianity. I. Woodwyk, Carissa. II. Title.
    HV875.T43 2011
    362.734 — dc23   2011028931

Cover design: Michelle Lenger
Cover imagery: Masterfile®, iStockphoto®

Printed in the United States of America

---

11 12 13 14 15 16 /DCI/ 26 25 24 23 22 21 20 19 18 17 16 15 14 13 12 11 10 9 8 7 6 5 4 3 2 1

Dedication

From Susan
To my three shining stars . . .
Matthew, Kola, and Lera

From Carissa
To my precious parents . . .
you may not have given me
physical life, but you taught me
how to live life, and for that
I am forever grateful.

Contents

Part III: Piecing It All Together

Foreword

Authors Susan TeBos and Carissa Woodwyk are inviting adoptive parents and kids on an adventure of a lifetime in *Before You Were Mine: Discovering Your Adopted Child's Lifestory*.

All adopted children, whether they are adopted domestically or internationally, have some sense of connection with their birth families. Adoption experts Drs. David M. Brodzinsky and Marshall Schechter say that the desire to search for a birth connection may not be a literal search, but it is a search nonetheless.

Why is a child's birth story so important? Many adoptees have questions and feel like something is missing: "Information is proof that I am a *real* person who was born at a *real* time and in a *real* place." The bottom line, however, is that adoptees need to know their lives are not a mistake.

For those with a missing or fragmented history, fulfilling the need for connection to their past can seem impossible. As an adopted person myself, my heart feels mysteriously bound to those adoptees and their parents who are trying to fulfill their children's need to know. Knowing the pieces of my birth story has brought fullness to my life and especially to who I am.

In my experience, answers came straight from the heart of God, through Scripture and prayer. Knowing our birth parents or where we were born is only the *physical* part of the story. The more exciting part is that we were born in the very heart of God himself, long before this world began. If the circumstances around our conception and birth were less than pleasant, we can remember what author Lee Ezell says, "Any two people can make love, but only God can create a life."[1] We are not mistakes, we are God's creations! We can base our self-esteem on what God says about us, that we are his jewels (Ez 16:4–7 TLB).

This book is unique because it gently weaves a biblical foundation throughout the center of every adopted child's story and emphasizes a child's life *before* he or she was adopted—a part of the story that is so often forgotten. It reaches the spirit and heals the hearts of adoptive parents and children.

Thanks to TeBos and Woodwyk for sharing the intimate parts of their adoption journeys, for keeping "His Story" exciting, and for providing such a practical tool for adoptees and parents to discover that they are a special part of the story!

— SHERRIE ELDRIDGE
AUTHOR OF *TWENTY THINGS ADOPTED KIDS*
WISH THEIR ADOPTIVE PARENTS KNEW

Introduction

Adoption ... the very word, spoken or unspoken, comes alive with deep meaning.

For every adoptive parent, there is a precious story of how a child entered his or her life. There is joy, celebration, responsibility, curiosity, and amazement. There is a sense that you are able to provide a kind of life for your adopted child that otherwise he or she may not have had.

But, we must remember, for every adopted child there is a story that is so often untold. There are loss, memories, history, questions, and people—missing people. Many feelings, shared or tucked away, are beneath the surface, undetected by even the closest observer.

> We, as parents, must become our child's storytellers.

Consider this ... What if adoption was an opportunity that God created to reveal himself through each adopted child's story? What if in the very act of receiving a child into our arms was an image of God receiving us into his arms? No judgment, no criticism, just pure love and acceptance. What if the very fragmented and broken pieces of our children's lives were put back together again and again?

Being adoptive parents challenges us to look deep within ourselves. It is a place of great discovery—about ourselves, about our child, and about God. Could it be that God would use the very thing that was so difficult for our child's birthmother and our child for good? Is that possible? We say, "Yes!" If God is a God who is about restoring *all* things, he must be passionate about restoring our child's missing pieces and his or her heart. So, as you discover your adopted child's lifestory in the pages of his or her Lifebook[1], may you bring hope, laughter, love, truth, imagination, and healing to your child's heart.

"Whoever welcomes one such child in my name welcomes me."

— MATTHEW 18:5

Overview

It was December 3, 1998, 10:30 p.m. Siberian time. My husband Mike and I had just traveled thirty hours to reach a large Siberian city, our final destination where we would soon adopt our first son, Matthew.

After spending the last two hours of our trip on a recycled Russian airliner, we were about to land on what appeared to be a runway of ice. Through our airplane window we caught a glimpse of the cold frosting the treetops. The darkness was extreme. We braced ourselves for a bumpy landing, but to our surprise it was as smooth as the ice beneath us, perhaps the best landing of the trip so far. We coasted for what seemed like miles on a hard-packed, icy runway and then stopped in the middle of nowhere. We were surprised when the pilots turned off the engines and casually exited the plane with a not so comforting farewell in Russian, "da svidanya," when translated—"until we meet again."

There we sat, nearly 200 bundled-up Russians and two very obvious Americans, in the dim glow of the emergency exit signs and lighting on the floor. Once our eyes adjusted, we could see the other passengers patiently waiting as if this was routine. "This would not go over well in the States," we thought. We were nervous and tired. Minutes felt like hours. "Finally!" we whispered to each other as the airplane hatch opened. But what were we so relieved about? Our adventure had just begun.

Upon exiting the plane, we were greeted by subzero temperatures as we walked to what we can only describe as frost-covered cattle cars hitched to tractors. No heat, no seats, just climb aboard and hold on. We were shuttled to the side exit gate of a modern looking airport terminal that appeared almost mysteriously out of the frosty night. Our adoption agency had instructed us to follow the other passengers no matter what. But the crowd was going outside the gate and no one was going inside the terminal. Silently, we kept cadence with the others. The hustle and bustle of the crowd kept us concealed for some time until we began to wonder if our contacts would ever find us. But once the crowd disappeared, we were finally spotted. It all unfolded just like a James Bond movie and, to our relief, the mission was going quite well.

Morning came and along with it the reality of the day's events. We were on an emotional high after months of preparing and waiting. Today would be the day we would meet our son for the first time. The dream of him had been all we needed to keep us going. We made our way to the city hospital where seven months earlier our son was born. Today, he was being cared for in the children's wing of that same hospital. Our final journey to meet him would take us over snow-covered, bumpy roads through the city. We had plenty of opportunities to take pictures and capture memories of the people and things going on around us, but our energy was fading and our memories alone would have to suffice. With camera, camcorder, and a list of questions still in hand we would try again as we hoped for a chance to take photos of our son and ask questions of his caregivers and doctor. We wanted to capture every priceless detail that we could.

But when the opportunity came, we put all that aside as the doctor gently placed a wiggly baby boy in our arms for the first time. We were so taken aback. He was so tiny. We had the chance of a lifetime to capture memories and stories about our precious son's beginnings, but instead our eyes were glued on this tiny dark-haired boy with crossed eyes who was sucking wildly on his binky (pacifier). We were mesmerized, and rightly so. He was the reason we had flown halfway around the world, braving vintage aircrafts flown by former Soviet pilots. Not knowing anything about Lifebooks[1] back then, we felt satisfied we had collected enough information about his birth history.

Months after returning home and settling into our new life as a family, I got busy reviewing my travel journal and other adoption documents that would help me piece together our son's adoption story. What I ended up with was a beautiful story about our adoption adventure and not a lot about our son's life prior to joining our family. At the time, I thought our son would be interested in how we became a family, our first bottle together, his first bath, and so forth. I had not considered how I would deal with the story of his birth, his separation from his birthmother, or how to honor his birth parents. Why? He was only a baby. What good would that information do anyhow? But soon I began to realize that the day would come when he would want to know and need to know the truth—the good things and the painful stuff. I wanted to be ready.

Who we are

We are Susan TeBos and Carissa Woodwyk.

I, Susan, am a wife and mother of three internationally adopted children. Before becoming a mom, I had a professional career, which I left to stay at home with our children. Whenever you see the pronoun "I" in this book, it refers to me. When I started the journey to write this book I set out thinking I had something new to say to other adoptive parents about Lifebooks. I thought I had learned a few new valuable lessons making my own children's Lifebooks and that I could share them with others interested in doing the same. It soon became much more than that. It became a faith walk and a huge lesson in being available for God's plan and not my own. I marvel at how he chose me to reveal his heart through this book. It was then that this book began to really take shape and focus. The intent was no longer just to teach parents how to make Lifebooks, but to open their eyes to the beauty of God's hand in their child's adoption and life and make him a part of their cherished story.

I, Carissa, am a wife and mother, a Korean-born adoptee, and a professional counselor. The invitation to cowrite this book with Susan was not only a surprise, but also an honor. As I entered more deeply into my lifestory, I realized even more that my birth story is one to celebrate and embrace. As a child, I grew up with very little information about my roots, my birth story, and the impact of my relinquishment. They were of little concern to me. But, as an adult, I have moved towards a fuller awareness of why knowing, believing, and accepting my birth story is vital to who I am. It is part of me, my heart, my life. So, as the words of my story became scattered throughout these pages, something amazing and transforming began to happen—I began to discover more of who I am and who God is calling me to be. It is a privilege to share this journey with you.

Together we have laughed, cried, pondered, wondered, researched, and spoken to hundreds of adoptive parents and adoptees while writing this book. Our lifestories, professional and personal knowledge, combined with our shared faith as believers in Jesus have helped us weave together a useful workbook for adoptive parents and adult adoptees that we believe is informative, challenging, and authentic. Every adopted child has a lifestory to discover, know, and understand. This book was written as a practical guide to equip you for your journey of discovery. Our hope is that you will find new information here that you may not have heard before, which will lead to new insights about your child's life before he or she was yours.

In an attempt to honor and respect the personal stories in this book, we have changed the names of parents and children.

What is in this book?

Every adopted child has a beginning. It starts long before the adventure we endured to hold them in our arms. It is often hard to remember that so many important things happened during the newborn, infant, and toddler stages even if we were not there to witness them. These events are special and will help provide us with answers for our adopted children as they wonder about what they were like and who they were with before joining our families.

We hope you selected this book because the topic not only caught your eye but hopefully your heart. If you are an adoptive parent looking for a Lifebook resource with practical advice and step-by-step guidance, this book can help. But, first and foremost, this book is not just another guide. It is much more than that. It is all about how you can discover and share your child's birth story and how it is intricately woven into God's story. This fresh, new way of thinking about Lifebooks will have a positive impact on your child's perception of her relinquishment and adoption for the rest of her life. It will be a gift because it is an important piece of her identity.

When we first began researching the concept of Lifebooks, we followed the advice of knowledgeable authors who had plenty of experience using them in the social work setting. Their solid advice and experience gave us a good reference for crafting our children's Lifebooks, to a certain extent. We include some of their advice in this book. When we began to teach Lifebook workshops, we started to design materials to make things easier for busy parents. It was in these workshops where we would get questions about how to include a Christian faith perspective so that our children could understand their birth history from God's perspective. How could we have missed this? After all, God knew our children long before we held them in our arms. He was there to witness their precious births. He held them close when it seemed their entire world was pushing them away or perhaps crashing in. While the grownups in their lives were unable to parent, God was.

While they stepped away for whatever crisis or cause, he stepped forward, carefully unfolding his plan. His character, unchanged throughout time, revealed his unfailing love, commitment, protection, and care for them. The process of restoring their hearts was beginning.

We were changed. And we forever changed our perspective on what a Lifebook should be. On the one hand we want to "front-load" our adopted children with the truth of their birth, as author Beth O'Malley explains.[2] On the other hand, we are invited to front-load that truth with God's truths about who they are.

Join us as we discover what is missing from our children's stories to create a Lifebook that is loaded with truth, faith, hope, and love. We will help you discover and claim God's faithfulness in the midst of your child's separation story and incorporate spiritual truths as only God can promise. The process will challenge you emotionally and move you to action as you develop a fresh new understanding of what a Lifebook can be for your child. Yet, at the same time, we will keep it simple, we promise. While some of you may feel inadequate to venture down this road of discovery, don't worry. We will guide you through the process with helpful questionnaires, offer relevant Bible verses you can claim for your child's specific situation, and suggest several ways you can pray for your child in ways specific to adoption matters.

The way we pray for an adopted child can be different and can make a difference in us as parents and in our relationship with God. As we have discovered, when you create and write a Lifebook for your child (and you), you will find plenty to pray about.

When you start this life-changing project, we suggest you ask God to give you wisdom (Jas 1:5) and understanding to see it through to completion. Parents, the more intentional you are now in laying a Christ-centered foundation throughout your child's story, the more he will be able to see God's hand in his birth, adoption, and future life circumstances. Wouldn't it be great to have your child look through his Lifebook pages and be filled with reassurance knowing you love him and God loves him too, no matter what brokenness may lie within his story?

Will a Lifebook be easy to write? It depends on your child's story and how willing you are to see it, sit with it, and embrace the truth of it. Our experience helping others plan and write Lifebooks has taught us that this process can be an emotional one for most if not all. For some parents it is the first time they realize their adopted child may hold inside herself hidden hurts from the reality of her relinquishment. A hurt so deep, as several adoption experts describe, that the pain often goes unspoken, unable to be put into words, and often showing up in unusual behaviors or attachment issues. When my husband and I first heard this, we thought, "How can it be? Our children are so happy." From what we could tell they were well adjusted and doing just fine. We could see no signs of pain or loss now nor did we anticipate any in the future. In hindsight, we were naïve. We now understand that every adopted child will process her adoption in her own way. Some will grieve and some will not. Some will ask questions and others will seem content. We will get into this later in the book. What is important is that they know they have a story and that it began at conception, not at adoption. Keep your eyes and heart open for the potential complicated emotions many adopted children hold hidden within. Be comforted by the positive way a Lifebook can be a door opener for adoption talk and how you can lead the way by becoming the storyteller.

Some parents may create a Lifebook for their children when they are young and others when their children are older. Learning how to be sensitive to your child's developmental age and level of understanding will make all the difference in helping him grasp difficult and potentially confusing information. For parents, knowing what to say, how to say it, and when to say it can also help reduce personal stress. For example, when our oldest son entered elementary school, I was uncomfortable telling him he had an older brother still living with his birthmother. For whatever reason, sharing this sensitive bit of information was stressful for me. What information do you have that will be stressful for you to tell? Having some guidelines can help better prepare us all for conversations like this and increase our confidence for any type of future adoption conversations. Therefore, we will introduce several guidelines to increase your confidence. We all will have difficult pieces of information to tell our children. Appropriate timing guidelines will make a difficult job much more doable.

Being in the trenches with busy parents has taught us a number of things. While parents often have the best intentions to create a Lifebook, the reality is that time is precious. And often, with lack of time comes frustration. Parents need good answers to the following questions:

Where do I begin?
What do I include?
What do I say?

If you are like us, busy parents with schedules, school, and bedtime routines, you will find answers to these questions in this book as well as an easy way to collect data, your thoughts, and get organized—all to help simplify the Lifebook process for you. We want to make the most of your time so that you will commit now to stay the course. In Part I, our hope is to help you capture the data you have scattered in files and boxes into a format that can easily be organized. Simplifying data collection is a time-effective tool that is very important to this multifaceted project. And while it is only one step, it is also half the battle. Part II of this book will talk about how to discover your child's story through questionnaires intended to get at the heart of the story. Finally, in the last section of this book, we will show you completed samples of Lifebook pages and give you easy "do-it-yourself" design ideas as a springboard for your own creativity. We will also suggest you take advantage of today's technology by going online and simply inserting the story you have written, the Scriptures you have carefully selected, and the photos and documents that bring your child's story alive into a ready-made format.

May the process of creating a Lifebook for your child be a representation of your steady, consistent, and faithful love—the same kind of love God demonstrates for his children. Let's get started!

PART I

The Difference Adoptive Parents Need to Know

Life can only be understood backwards, but it must be lived forwards.

— SØREN KIERKEGAARD

CHAPTER 1

What a Lifebook Is and Is Not

You will often find me at my headquarters, seated at a small red plastic Playschool picnic table, strategically located in the middle of our kitchen. This is prime real estate that I share with our preschooler's Play-doh and paint supplies and where I keep in touch with our on-the-go kids. It is rarely quiet at our house. With piano practice, wrestling matches, glamorous makeovers, or our three-year-old daughter helping our husky six-year-old son get in touch with his feminine side—we are a busy family. Our three kids are just like many kids. They are happy, growing, and learning about who they are.

Because all three of our children are adopted, we have a strong desire to help them learn more about who they are. It is through the stories in their Lifebooks that they get a glimpse of where they were born, what their lives were all about before they joined ours, and where we get a window into how they are feeling about what they are learning. If one of our children wants to look at his Lifebook, all other siblings show up, too—with big ears, big eyes, and often big questions. Since all of our children were adopted at different times, their stories are all different. But they have one big thing in common. They know they are our children and God's children, too. What a great beginning, but there is so much more.

Chosen by God and precious.

—1 PETER 2:4

Family photo albums and scrapbooks

How many of you have prepared photo albums or scrapbooks that hold cherished stories of your family? They are collections of memories that tell us where we have been as a family, how we spend our time together, and what we hold dear. They honor past generations, highlight celebrations, such as a new baby's arrival, and showcase accomplishments with mementoes such as report cards and sports awards.

In our family, our scrapbooks send our children excitedly down memory lane full of joy as they reminisce about family trips to Florida, student-of-the-month awards, class field trips, our cousin's annual pool party, or camping at Sand Lake. Their memories fill them with happiness, a sense of family, and love. In contrast, how many family scrapbooks are filled with, well, not-so-good memories? Oh, I have been tempted to include stories of the potty training blues, sibling rivalry, stitches, broken bones, broken hearts, poor eating habits, painful car rides—need I say more?

Remembering the good times and forgetting the not-so-good times just comes naturally. Perhaps that is one of the reasons that putting together a book of memories about a child's life prior to adoption, a Lifebook, doesn't always come so naturally. In fact, for some, it can be quite uncomfortable. And with good reason. On the one hand there is often missing information, or difficult information, or perhaps not enough information. On the other hand, there may be a story of loss, perceived rejection, and potential confusion. Instead of sending our children down memory lane filled with joy as we do with our family photo albums, we with uncertainty send them down an unpaved road of memories when we share a Lifebook—one that may seem bumpy, a bit jarring, and sometimes scary at first. And yet this road must be traveled, with child close by our side, to lovingly clarify confusion, to confront and validate grief, to sensitively honor their past, and for us to join in on the healing of past hurt. As with most travel, it is best to be prepared.

The difference adoptive parents need to know

The good news is we do not have to make this trip alone. We have a compassionate Heavenly Father who is able (Dn 3:17) to do immeasurably more than all we can ask or imagine (Eph 3:20). We do not have to rely on our own power. He has a story to tell through our child as well. A Lifebook is not without joy!

It is a celebration of the miracle of your child's birth: "Before I started to put you together in your mother, I knew you" (Jer 1:5 NLV).

It is a reminder of God's constant care and love for her: "I will never leave you. I will never abandon you" (Heb 13:5a TEV).

It is the promise of a life filled with hope: "I will bless you with a future filled with hope — a future of success, not of suffering" (Jer 29:11 CEV).

Can we forget God's heart and his side of the story?

One adoptive mom sent me an email one day when she discovered what was missing from her daughter's Lifebook. I will share the short version with you. "I'm finishing up my daughter's Lifebook as I'm writing this. I'm so glad it's done and she's so excited! It does need a little something. Do you have a list of Scripture that pertains to adoption? Could I have a copy? That's what this Lifebook is lacking." Purposefully filling the gaps of our children's birth story with God's pictures and truths is important. It will bring meaning and fullness to a Lifebook.

There is so much more to come to show you how to bring fullness to your child's story as the pages of this book unfold. First, let's take a quick look at what a Lifebook is all about, its benefits, what adopted children want to know, and some guidelines for its use. Then we will move on to chapter 2 and discover how sharing your faith fits in.

What is a Lifebook?

Let's begin with a basic overview of what a Lifebook is and then talk about what a Lifebook is not. There are a few important distinctions worth knowing that will be helpful when you complete a Lifebook and begin sharing it with your child.

A Lifebook is a story book that acknowledges, celebrates, explains, and honors the life of an adoptee prior to adoption. It gathers the bits and pieces of our adopted children's lives before they joined our families and gracefully organizes it all — words, pictures, documents, and photos — in the form of a story. The good stuff, like babies' "firsts," are fun to document because all children love to see photos and hear stories about themselves. In some cases you may be surprised to learn some children just need to know they were born. The sad or painful stories are shared with sensitivity and without omitting any truths.

Such stories may include the reason your child was separated from his birthmother and birthfather and any other identifying details about them. It is important to hear the words "before joining our family" because parents often forget it is this important distinction that makes a Lifebook unique.

A traditional Lifebook has its roots or foundation in social work and psychology. Professionals from these fields initially identified the need of adopted children for something tangible to hold onto that connected them to their beginnings. Lifebooks have been used for years in the United States foster care system. Only in recent years has the idea evolved and is now being used by adoptive families. Psychologists and social workers have the background to understand a Lifebook's impact on an adopted child. They agree that this simple concept has positive, lifelong benefits for both your child and you. Following is a list of reasons why creating a Lifebook is important.

"You are actively contributing to their emotional well-being by shaping how they will view their beginnings."[1]

— CINDY PROBST

Lifebook benefits

 A Lifebook may help children in the following ways:

Offers a "safe" tool children can use to think, discuss, question, and grieve their beginnings.

Makes their story feel "real" by having it all written down.

Reinforces "It's not your fault."

Reduces birth parent fantasies.

Prevents children from making up their own reasons for their adoption.

Reduces uncertainty about their past.

Helps develop a sense of self (identity formation).

Encourages a child to discover and imagine.

Normalizes a child's birth story.

Gives a child a history to embrace.

The Lifebook process may help parents in the following ways:

Helps parents formulate answers for tough questions before they are asked.

Guides parents through phrasing sad or painful information.

Reinforces healthy parent/child bond and fosters attachment and trust.

Establishes an open door communication policy.

Helps create confidence because the story is well rehearsed.

Gives parents the opportunity to know, validate, and embrace their child's birth story.

What a Lifebook is not

There are some unique differences that make a Lifebook highly personal and therefore more private than perhaps the adoption trip album. Let's take a look at what a Lifebook is *not* and share a few guidelines at the same time.

A Lifebook is *not* typically a collection of notes or documents from your adoption dossier. Nor is it a scrapbook of airline ticket stubs, visa photos, or baby shower memories. We have discovered after talking with adoptive moms that many are so afraid to throw anything away. They arrive at workshops with boxes and binders full, not knowing where to begin. The good news is that for this project you will be able to put most of those keepsakes away somewhere safe. This is your child's lifestory prior to adoption and not his or her adoption story. Look for tips later in the book on how to transition your child's story to include that special story when you became a family.

A Lifebook is *not* a book you or your child will share with casual acquaintances. While not meant to be secretive in any way, it is a personal keepsake full of private memories and stories that should only be shared with others with discretion. Your child will have some say in who views his Lifebook, but help him set boundaries that will protect his heart and story.

We received a telephone call one day from an adoptive mom with two Korean-born children. She described her son's first experience being caught off guard with questions from inquisitive classmates about his adoption. His tears signaled not only his hurt, but also some confusion. He did not know what to say to them. Mom fortunately had completed his Lifebook and pulled it from the shelf and they snuggled together reading his birth story. At seven years old, he was ready to understand many of the details in his story. He also felt something special about the love and support of his mom, whose lap he was sitting on. But he still was not sure how to respond to his classmates. Mom and son agreed on what they would share from his Lifebook and together returned to school a few days later to give the class an important opportunity to learn about how some families are made through adoption.

A Lifebook does *not* contain sugarcoated truths. While our son's and daughter's lives may have begun in ways we could not imagine or want for them, they still deserve and need to hear the truth. This can be a hard thing to swallow for some parents. Our natural instincts are to protect our children from hurt. What good could possibly come from telling our sons or daughters something that may cause them pain? But the reality is, according to bonding and attachment expert Dr. Gregory Keck, healing comes from telling the truth. Secrets, half-truths, and full omissions can only lead to broken trust and relational damage between you and your child. When a lifestory does not make sense, an adopted child is forced to make one up, according to authors Keefer and Schooler in their book, *Telling the Truth to Your Adopted or Foster Child.* They further warn, "Often, the adopted child's self-esteem is more damaged by silence or deceit than by reality."[2]

"Reality is the best option. Even bad news is good news because it is real news."[3]

— RON NYDAM

At one Lifebook workshop, an adoptive mom shared a very common story with the group that evening. She and her husband had adopted a beautiful little girl from Eastern Europe. She revealed her husband's secret desire to destroy the painful story that unfolded in the written pages of their daughter's adoption documents. He could not bring himself to cause his little girl emotional pain. He could not see past the painful details and felt concealing them forever would be the safer route. However, secrets rarely remain that way. In his efforts to protect his daughter in this way, he was assuming the risk of damaging their relationship and foundation of trust in the future, should the secret be exposed. As parents, it is not our responsibility to prevent pain, but rather to walk alongside our children and love them as they experience pain.

By discouraging communication about the topic of relinquishment, parents are giving up an important opportunity to build trust and positively influence their child's understanding of who she is. It was not so long ago when families seldom spoke of or celebrated their child's birth history. The adoption story may have been told on occasion; however, the birth story and relinquishment were seldom told, fragmented, and typically not written down. Not only were adopted children unable to explore their stories and emotions together with the loving support of a parent, they were missing out on the story of hope that can only come when we include our faith. Imagine a mom and dad assuming there was no point, no reason or benefit in "dredging up the past." Imagine the adopted sons or daughters silently wondering about their birth families, trying to make sense of something that seemed so confusing. Many adoptees from that era are adults today still wondering with mixed emotions how to approach the topic of their birth history with their adoptive family and resolve unanswered questions of loss. There are missing pieces to every adopted child's life. Not one adopted child escapes this truth. Not yours, not mine. For some parents, they want to hide the truth. For others, it may be that they do not know they need to tell the truth. Just consider some of the most common questions or missing pieces adopted children wish they knew the answers to, as told to a social worker and reprinted in an adoption support magazine.[4]

What are my birth parents' first and middle names?

Where was I born (hospital and city)?

What time was I born?

Did my birthmother see me or hold me?

Who was present at my birth?

Did my birthmother know anything about my adoptive family?

Did my birthmother name me?

Does anyone else in my birth family know about me?

Was I in a foster home?

How old were my birth parents when I was born?

Were they married? Did they marry each other or anyone else after I was born?

Where did my birth parents go to high school? College?

What kind of students were they?

What traits did I inherit from my birth parents?

What is my medical history?

What religious background do my birth parents have?

Are my birth parents still alive?

Do they love me?

Do they think about me?

Would they ever want to speak to me or meet me?

Why we need to tell

Adopted children need constant reassurance that who they are matters, and that comes from retelling their story time and again. Author and adult adoptee Sherri Eldridge advises parents to "compassionately engage your child in conversation that fosters identification and encourages verbalization of her feelings and needs. Here healing begins."[5] A Lifebook is a tool for parents to use that will help encourage healing from any effects of relinquishment. A Lifebook also helps children to know it is acceptable to love and care about two sets of parents. Authors Keefer and Schooler confirm this by writing, "Permission to know about, and care about, his birth family actually frees a child to know and care about his adoptive family."[6]

For many adopted children, hearing their stories — including the difficult parts — is a relief. Yet, others may be indifferent or have minimal interest. Since every person responds and adapts to loss differently, the key is to be aware of all possible reactions and be ready to support your child no matter what may surface. My husband and I anticipate that each of our three children will respond to their stories in ways as unique as they are. While our approach will be consistent in many ways, it will be flexible in others. The one-size-fits-all theory from decades past is no longer an option.

Finally, the process of making a Lifebook will become your dress rehearsal time as you develop the details of the story. While you sift through delicate information and think through any challenging circumstances you will become so familiar with your son's or daughter's story that, if or when tough questions surface, you will be better prepared and less likely to be caught off guard. Children wonder about their adoption more than we think, according to the experts. Becoming your child's expert resource will boost your ability to respond to questions more confidently, allow you to become more proactive introducing the topic of adoption, and will show your child that you care about his life before he became yours.

In the next chapter, we will continue looking at ways to develop your child's story. Through the eyes of compassion we will see how God's heart brings fullness and how every detail belongs to him, including relinquishment and adoption details. As the storyteller, you will learn how vital your role is for supporting your child through the many stages of understanding. Let's continue learning about the powerful difference between a traditional Lifebook and one rooted in faith and how you can be used in a powerful way by God in your role as storyteller.

"May the God who gives
endurance and encouragement
give you the same attitude of
mind toward each other that
Jesus Christ had."

— ROMANS 15:5

HOMEWORK

creating sharing	Discuss with your spouse or a trusted friend how you feel about creating and sharing a Lifebook with your adopted child.
telling	Discuss together how you feel about telling your son or daughter *all* of his/her birth story.
start the process	What is scary, exciting, and/or challenging? What do you need before you start this process?

The words that are spoken by the most important people in our lives paint the most important pictures for our lives.[1]

— JOHN BURNS

CHAPTER 2

Becoming the Storyteller

Our children love to go to the YMCA to play. Whether it is to swim, rock climb, or just venture into the kid's center full of crafts and climbing toys, the experience is a favorite for them. On one occasion we were stopping in briefly so that I could work out and the kids could play when our son Nickolai wandered over to a table scattered full of odds and ends of wood pieces. Never had he laid eyes on such a wonderful assortment of shapes and sizes. And there was glue too. Not just household glue, but carpenter's glue. It was all so inviting and yet overwhelming at the same time. He turned to me and grabbed my hand, signaling he was not sure he knew what to do. With a little encouragement and a few ideas from mom, he began taking pieces that did not make sense alone and began building something very special.

> Parents, sometimes we have to sit
> in the middle of things to figure
> out how they go together.

When Nickolai proudly displayed his supersonic bat plane complete with rocket launcher to me, I could see he had put a lot of thought into carefully placing and gluing each piece. As the glue dried, occasionally a piece would fall off and we would scoop it up off the floor and reset it. After all, the plane would have a hard time flying without one of its wings.

When I think of this story, I am reminded of the topics that we will discuss in this chapter. I think of the inviting yet overwhelming task of creating a Lifebook and yet, with a little encouragement, desire outweighs doubt. I see the scattered pieces of wood as pieces of our child's story and God's story and how they fit together to make something special. And I think of the glue that holds it all together. How much stronger things are once the glue is firmly set. After all, how can one fly without wings firmly set?

As we move to building a future of understanding for our children, we will need to learn how the pieces go together so we can share something special that will help our children soar confidently into adulthood.

Faith stories

Our children's adoptions were life-changing events that we believe God played a part in and continues to play a part in today. His fingerprints are everywhere. He is not far and elusive as some may think or believe (Heb 4:12 – 13). He is close and active in this world today. God was not surprised when our children were born into this world. The miracle of life belongs to him. He is the creator of life. He is the God who sees (Ps 139:16 TLB). Therefore we should not be surprised when he responds to their situation and makes it something good. "Faith sees the invisible, believes the unbelievable, and receives the impossible."[2] We believe our children are with us today because God responded to their need and our desire to parent them. It is a faith story we cherish. A faith story we will tell.

We discover a precious piece of God's heart through his response to adoption. He is the defender of the fatherless, not the cause. We can help our children understand who God is and what his character is all about in an attempt to encourage a fuller understanding of who he is.

Looking back on chapter 1, we discovered the many important benefits that creating and sharing a traditional Lifebook can offer. In this chapter we will build on those benefits and make an essential connection to the spiritual needs of our children. Children are spiritual and often their greatest needs are spiritual, too. As adoptive parents transfer their faith to a new generation, they are helping to shape their children's perceptions of God, self, others, and the world. When we help our adopted children see and understand a piece of their identity, they are better able to discover and believe their value in God's eyes. And that is the message we hope to send to parents throughout the rest of this book. That our children have great value, worth, and purpose in our eyes — and God's eyes too. Our prayer is that their Life-books will reflect this.

We depart from a traditional Lifebook here, not at a crossroads, but through a merging of both, taking with us everything we need from a traditional Lifebook and including God's side of the story, too. We now become treasure hunters looking for gold — but not just the gold found in the facts and data in our child's documents, as important as that is, but also the gold found in Scripture that we can intimately tie to our child's unique adoption experience. The Bible says we are to saturate our children with an awareness of the Lord (Dt 6:4–9). Imagine sharing your child's birth heritage while at the same time introducing her to her spiritual heritage. Connecting the two not only brings fullness to the story, but can help us send messages that shape our child's perception of her birth story, her relinquishment, and who she is in Christ and who she is to become. Further, for children who may be grieving their relinquishment, it can begin the process of healing.

In Part II of this book, we will show you how to weave Scripture promises throughout your child's Lifebook. We give you plenty of help by providing relevant lists of Scripture so that you may personalize a prayer, a verse, or a promise for your child. And, yes, prayer will become an important part of what we do in this book. "Prayer is a part of our God-given urge to protect, care for, and shape the precious children he has given us."[3]

What message do you want to send?

We believe an adopted child will someday benefit from aligning her perception of herself with how God sees her. We anticipate her attitudes and decisions will be positively influenced as well. As a matter of fact, all children can benefit, especially in today's world where negative messages seem to outweigh the positive ones. Messages that may be convincing enough for a child to believe she is second best, a mistake, not good enough, bad, at fault or flawed somehow, rejected, and more. How important it becomes for our messages to them to be filled with acceptance, purpose, and hope. Hopefully, if we tell our children they matter, have value and purpose, then as they grow they will eventually believe it. Not at age four but perhaps at age fourteen when they are forming their own identities apart from us.

Going beyond the given

Our children's Lifebooks are full of facts and safe assumptions of their births and the circumstances surrounding the separation and relinquishment from their families of origin. But they became even fuller when we began considering something special that we did not find in the collection of papers in their adoption files. We turned to Scripture and found verse after verse of promises that we could claim for each of our children. It became clear that, while our children may have been unplanned by their birth parents for one reason or another, they were not unplanned by God. Author Rick Warren captivated me when he wrote in his book, *The Purpose Driven Life,* "God never does anything accidentally, and He never makes mistakes. He has a reason for everything He creates."[4] Can you imagine how I felt as an adoptive mom when I connected these truths to our children's stories? While we have poured out our love on our children in so many ways, Scripture says God pours out even more (1 Jn 3:1). While our children know how special they are to us, Scripture says they are even that much more special to God (Mt 19:14). My heart melts when I personalize verses with the names of our children. "I am your Creator. You, Nickolai, Lera, Matthew, were in my care even before you were born" (Is 44:2 CEV). As important as the facts and data are for our children to know in light of their birth stories, we believe our children need to learn this, too. Their Lifebook pages seemed like the perfect place. Where else would they revisit their personal stories over and over, year after year? We wanted to take advantage of these teachable moments hoping the connection would someday bring a sense of belonging, peace, and amazement that the God who sees (Eph 1:4–5) responded to their needs and brought them to the very place they belonged—in our family. We will never be able to fix their fragmented beginnings. We may never have all the answers they will want or need, but we can offer a message of hope in the midst of it all so that one day they may understand God's heart for them, his response to their loss, and his plan for their future. Does this alter the story? No. Does this make a fresh connection that will positively shape how our children perceive the story of who they are? We believe the answer is, "Yes."

Shaping and connecting

As mentioned earlier, we believe your child will someday benefit from aligning her perception of herself with how God sees her. Helping shape our children's perceptions of themselves, others, and the world is what we do as parents on a daily basis. Consider safety for example. Most, if not all, of us begin impressing safety messages upon our children within months of their birth. Almost as if on auto pilot, we take each new little recruit by the hand, guiding him, talking with him, showing him, and preparing him so that he does not put himself in harm's way. Safety messages are simple at first, but no less important. They lay a foundation for understanding, both in the present and future. As our children grow, the safety messages do not stop. As a matter of fact, they advance, and new important safety messages emerge: messages regarding relationships, drugs, and driving—just to name a few. Should we neglect to share safety messages at various stages in our children's lives, we are leaving important safety matters to chance. The point is that we have a unique privilege to shape our children's understanding of many important things as they grow and prepare to become adults. The same is true for how we help shape our children's perceptions of who they are in light of their relinquishment, separation, and adoption.

Becoming the storyteller

Many adopted children may never get a firsthand account of why they were relinquished, so the stories we tell may be the only glimpse they will ever get of their lives prior to adoption. For a child, not knowing her story or being invited to talk about it removes her ability to see and understand the full picture of who she is and God's full redemptive plan for her life. Our job as storyteller then becomes essential. In many big and small ways our children's stories provide more than facts and historical data. They provide insight, dispel lies, set the record straight, introduce human frailty, open wounds, and satisfy longings. A child is not prepared to navigate her story alone. The privilege then is ours.

Let's take a look at what it means to become the storyteller, and what it means to proactively participate in helping our children gain a healthy understanding of who they are.

Below and on the next page are several suggestions for parents who wish to become their child's storyteller.

Invest time	**Get comfortable** with your child's story.
	"Many children rarely raise the subject of adoption themselves," caution Keefer and Schooler. "When some children ask questions about adoption, they pick up cues that the topic is uncomfortable for the adoptive parent and should be avoided in the future."[5]
Be approachable	**Build trust** and create a safe environment.
Be proactive	Our child's relinquishment is not a topic of daily discussion, but we can look for "everyday" opportunities to **share and encourage** questions. We will never have to have the "big talk" if we are having it continuously in bits and pieces and building understanding as we go about life.
Dig deep	See yourself as more than a giver of facts. Look beyond the facts and data to **uncover unique insights**.
	Through the eyes of compassion, can you uncover the story behind the story?
	Can you safely read between the lines of your child's adoption documents? For example, can you discover a character trait or traits of a birth parent that could lend some insight?
	Or, could you identify human frailty in the midst of your child's abandonment or placement (without excusing behavior) that may help set the record straight?
Allow emotions to surface	A Lifebook will stir up emotions. Watch and listen as your child takes the lead in discovering her story.
	Celebrate her birth when she celebrates.
	Honor her feelings of being relinquished whether good or bad.
	Know her heart's desires and concerns.
	Love her unconditionally.

Dispel lies	We believe the deceiver (Satan) can gain a foothold through our child's vulnerabilities instilling lies such as, "You are not worthy" or "You are not good enough" or "You are too much to handle."
	Correcting a child's feelings and beliefs of unworthiness or shame due to misinformation or not knowing can help **shape healthy perceptions and beliefs** about birth parents and relinquishment. This clarifies to the child that he is not at fault.
Be sensitive	**Understand** your child's developmental readiness for information. Like the pot boiling on the stove, parents know what is too hot to handle well before the child does. We will discuss this more in chapter 3.
Evaluate beliefs	Look for opportunities to **share your values**.
	"Children raised with a set of values different from their birth parents may also find it difficult to forgive the 'sins' of the past," according to Carolyn Macinnes.
	"Through Lifebooks, parents can provide compassionate explanations about the birth parents' decisions while empowering children to make wise choices in their own lives."[6]
Have your radar on	Be alert for opportunities to connect your child's past, present, and future with God's truths. Adoptive parents have a special opportunity to **leave a faith imprint** on their children by developing a fuller story of God's involvement in their lives and to teach them to lean on the strength of their Creator who wants to lavish upon them more than we can possibly imagine.

As you enter into your child's story it will become important for you to claim God's promises for her. There are many faith messages and many ways to share your faith. We have selected several essential messages God has for our adopted children that we can purposefully share with them in everyday conversations and our adoption conversations. But do not let our suggestions limit you. In their book, *Parents' Guide to the Spiritual Growth of Children*, John Trent[7] (*et al.*) offers an extensive list that we cannot begin to fully include here. So, if you are interested in additional resources on the topic of sharing your faith with your child, refer to the resources in the back of this book.

> God created you. (Ps 139:16 CEV)
>
> God loves you. (Rom 8:38–39)
>
> God wants to take care of you. (Is 44:2a CEV)
>
> God has a plan for you. (Jer 29:11 NCV)
>
> God will never leave you. (Rom 8:38–39 or Dt 31:6)
>
> God is faithful. (Dt 7:9, 1 Cor 1:9, 2 Thes 3:3)
>
> God delights in you. (Ps 35:27b)
>
> God's word is true. (2 Tm 3:16–17 or 2 Pt 1:20–21)
>
> God is with you. (Heb 13:5b–6, Rom 8:28)

"God has always made a point of honoring those who start out and are faithful in using the 'few things' that He has given them."[8] So start with these beautiful basics that are a reflection of God's love and that most never tire of hearing. They are simple and easy enough to whisper in the ear of a sleepy child or to wonder in awe as you dream together of what the future holds. God becomes more real to our children when they see and hear about his desires and activity in their lives. Perhaps you have your own ways of sharing your faith — a special song, poems, small notes tucked in special places like a shoe or under a pillow. Now you can include them in the pages of your child's Lifebook.

> Every chance, every whisper,
> every note, becomes the "glue" for
> our children's wings.

We have discovered that by knowing these truths, believing them, and being alert to opportunities to share them, we are sharing them more often than we ever expected. We trust that if we deliver the messages God promises to our children, the Holy Spirit will do the rest (Phil 2:13, 1:6).

"Mom and Dad, planting the seeds
of Biblical truths is your job,
making them bud and grow is
God's."9

Some final thoughts

As you interact with your child and talk with her about her story, what messages will you send? How will you explain why your child is with you today? How will you make sense of a crisis pregnancy, or adoption laws that force abandonment of babies, or extreme poverty that cannot feed, clothe, or care for one more, or a reckless lifestyle where children are removed for their own safety, or a birthmother's choice in love to secure her child a healthy future?

As you continue to discover all God has for your child, how much he loves her, how he created her for a purpose, how he will take care of her, how his plan will continue to unfold in her life, and how he will never leave her, our prayer is that while you sit in the middle of things sorting out how they go together to make something special, God will meet you there. May he elevate in your heart the desire and importance to become the storyteller.

It was not good fortune that
responded to the needs of our
children when their first parents
could not parent, it was our
Creator.

"Behold, I make all things new."

— REVELATION 21:5 NKJV

HOMEWORK

sharing	In what ways are you currently sharing God's heart with your child?
faith messages	What faith messages can you begin sending to your child now? What faith messages will you include in your child's Lifebook that will display God's hand in his/her lifestory in the past, present, and future?
list benefits	List some benefits of becoming the storyteller—for you and for your child.

Timing is God's way of making sure
everything doesn't all happen at
once.

— UNKNOWN

CHAPTER 3

Avoiding Information Overload

Overjoyed, relieved, and victorious would best describe how I felt the day I finally finished our first son's Lifebook. Overjoyed because I had completed an important gift that would have true purpose in my child's life, relieved because I finally felt better prepared to help him understand this piece of his identity, and victorious because I had persevered when so many other things could have gotten in the way. I had poured my heart into it, anticipating the day I would lovingly give our son this gift and he would attentively hang on every word. Overjoyed and reveling in my victory, I could not wait to share it with him. Perhaps one would say I was a bit fanatical. (Webster's would describe me as excessively enthusiastic and devoted.) My son would describe me as nuts. It was a memorable day indeed! I will never forget his reaction as I marched him through each page, pointing out every detail. He was disinterested and downright bored. Not exactly the reaction I had expected. As he pushed off my lap to go play, I will never forget my reaction. I was bewildered. (Webster's would call me confused.) I would call me nuts! Sitting in the dust of my son's quick beeline back to his toys, I thought to myself, "What was I thinking? He's four! His heart is with his toys." He was no more ready for the information I had to share than I was to give it. My timing, my approach—it was all wrong.

This experience taught me well. It was time to regroup. After commiserating with a friend, to my relief, I found I was not alone. Sarah, an adoptive mom of two little boys from Guatemala, had her own story to tell of a botched first attempt at sharing a Lifebook with one of her children.

Sarah had just completed her oldest son's Lifebook after months of working on this labor of love. She had crafted each page beautifully and selected each word carefully. Finally, she was ready and confident to share with him the precious photos and stories of his birth. Sarah describes placing her three-year-old son on her lap to look through his book together. She was about to enter uncharted territory that not even her training in social work had prepared her for. She could not predict how her son would respond to what he was about to hear. The first page proudly displayed a black-and-white photo of her son's Guatemalan birthmother. "This is Guadalupe. This is your birthmother," she began. And that is as far as she got. Her son was stunned. His reaction? A huge surprise. Ever since Sarah and her husband had met their son's birthmother during one of their adoption trips to Guatemala, a rare and priceless opportunity many of us will not get, they felt confident he should know about her. But when her son saw the photo and heard the word birthmother, he turned to her searching her eyes asking, "Aren't you my mother?" Not once, not twice, but over and over in a confused and frightened way.

Sarah knew then it was all too soon. She closed his Lifebook and scooped him up in her arms and spent the next several days reassuring his searching mind and heart that she indeed was his true mother. The Lifebook found itself on a shelf in time-out — a cooling off period followed and a chance for Sarah to learn more about the impact of a Lifebook and how timing plays such an important role.

What seemed so right ended up so wrong

Experience is often the best teacher, but sometimes the toughest, too. Unfortunately, we cannot guarantee that you will not find yourself in an awkward moment just as we did. It is humbling to say the least. This is just as much of a learning process for us as it is for you and your children. Yet these first experiences begin the process of opening doors that can lead you and your child through beneficial and, at times, challenging but necessary conversations. Thankfully, children have forgiving hearts and we can count on that during those first attempts when we might stumble.

We have this wonderful parental privilege, unlike any other, that is unique to the adoptive family experience: to plan, prepare, rehearse, and present a truthful birth story to our adopted children. However, in order for it all to make sense we need to understand our children's hearts and consider their ability to understand their stories at different developmental stages of their lives. While our mistakes were eye opening, they set us off on a course to discover more about child development and how children process information as they grow.

In this chapter we will help you understand, or maybe just remind you, that all adopted children will have different concerns, different questions, different speeds of learning and desires to know, or not to know, their stories. God, in his amazing wisdom, created our children to have distinctive developmental windows of understanding. This means our keen, little bright-eyed children will only understand so much at a given age. As they grow, their understanding grows.

He also gave them emotions that can rise to the surface in many different ways—through tears, behaviors, attitudes, and indifference, to name a few. These and more act as indicators that help guide us in our interaction *with* them. We, as storytellers, need to learn how to use our children's Lifebooks with them as they grow and change, so the story we tell is age appropriate and the words we speak captivate them on their own level.

Where do we begin? First, we will briefly review the four stages of learning each child grows through. These developmental stages will act as our guide, reminding us to tell a simple story to the youngest child and build on that story as she grows. But, remember, you know your child best. For example, we know with our children chronological age is not always the most accurate measure of maturity. What do you know about your child that might lead you to believe she is ready or not so ready? Second, we will suggest a few tips to help you make your child's Lifebook grow with her for years to come.

A quick review

Children move through four developmental stages. These stages of understanding include preschool, early elementary, middle school, and early adolescence. While preschoolers *could* understand being adopted, they really don't. They enjoy the "show and tell" of their story, as they would any story, and it begins a good foundation for future understanding.

Around six years old, they *do* begin to understand. Not everything, not yet. For instance, children at this stage do not understand rape, mental illness, prostitution, or abject poverty. So it is best to "limit negative details."[1] But, while starting to think rationally at this stage about adoption, with his emerging ability to think abstractly, a child's black-and-white thinking still makes him susceptible to blaming himself for his relinquishment. Therefore, it is good from time to time to check and correct perceptions a child may have arrived at incorrectly.

Let's take a look at how this was done by one adoptive mom. An eight-year-old boy told his mother he thought his birthmother just gave him away with no thought, concern, or love. In this case the child had a misperception that needed correcting, but mom waited. He then told her he did not like his birthmother, even called her some names like "stupid" and "crazy," words he might use to express his frustration with his siblings, but this time he used to express his frustration with his birthmother. Mom still waited. Finally, after the child contemplated some more, mom listened as he expressed a positive desire to want to communicate with his birthmother, perhaps even through email. Hmm!

How important it was for this mom to let this child experience his emotions — to quietly wait, to show her support through listening, to remain near and not abandon him, and to let him know it was okay to talk about it instead of dismissing it. This is exactly what a child needs at this stage — a listening ear, affirming love, and correct information. It is also a good time to explain how love can and does coexist with sadness and hurt. This will go on for awhile and then, finally, in early adolescence and beyond, children are able to process information that seems contrary to common sense yet may be true. Self-discovery is in full swing. Close, consistent support will be vital. Let's take a look how this all applies to a Lifebook.

Preschool

Vera Fahlberg, who has written extensively and with obvious expertise on the topic of adoption, suggests the following way to share a Lifebook with a preschool child. For children under age four, "Parents may use an adopted child's Lifebook much as they would a baby book."[2]

Do you remember your own preschool and kindergarten days when "show and tell" gave you a chance to talk about something that was important to you? This approach gives parents the chance to show and tell their child her precious story — to delight in her firsts, to awe over her signature tuft of hair, to be captivated by the miracle of who she is. It is a chance to use a full range of emotions to bring fullness to her story. To describe her, but to describe mom and dad too — happy, surprised, sad, nervous, relieved, thankful. It is also a chance to begin introducing the faith messages that speak of the Father's heart about her birth and shaping her perceptions of who she is and what she will eventually believe about herself.

As you relate the facts of your child's story rather than read them systematically (a big error in my first attempt), your preschooler will more likely enjoy her Lifebook and seek it out in the future with this approach. While we suggest you write her story with a beginning, middle, and an end, at a young age your child does not need to have it read to her from start to finish or word for word. Let your child lead. Watch her and then let her watch you. For a little one, you will know you have done well if she is captivated by what she sees and hears. For example, to represent the weather on the day our first son was born (it is amazing what you can find on the Internet) we caught his attention with a beautiful, bright yellow sun. We also have displayed colorful maps that act as a great conversation starter. The point is, let creativity be your guide.

Early elementary

If you have set the tone in the preschool years and have established an environment that is open and safe for adoption talk, early-elementary-school-age children will have a good foundation to "assist them in developing positive attitudes about adoption, their birth parents, and themselves ..."[3] We have discovered in the early elementary years that our two boys present a much more sophisticated line of questioning than our preschool daughter. Our oldest son went from an attitude of indifference to one of casual interest, asking questions like, "What does she look like?" "How old is she?" "How big is my birth city?" At this age a child is ready for our most basic answers to why and how. And while they hear the words we say, they are still mastering their meaning. It is all a part of building trust, opening communication between us, and furthering their understanding. It is good to practice.

It is also a good time for listening to a child's perceptions on relinquishment and adoption matters and correcting any misperceptions before moving on.[4] As with all children, repeating, listening, re-explaining, and processing are essential steps in forming a healthy understanding of new concepts.

From show and tell to concrete thinker to correcting perceptions, a Lifebook takes on new meaning at every stage.

Middle school

Whether you have been the storyteller for your child since the beginning or are just entering at this stage, your middle school child, according to the experts, is ready to hear the details of her story beyond the basic descriptions. And according to the authors of *The Complete Book of Baby and Child Care* from Focus on the Family, your school age child's eyes and ears and heart are likely to be as open to your input as they will ever be in her life. "Once she begins adolescence, this will probably not be the case—at least for a while."[5] Invite your child to sit with you and read through her Lifebook. Listen to what she says, observe her expressions and feelings, and check interpretations. Beth O'Malley writes, "It is always a good idea to ask your child directly why she thinks she is no longer with the birth family."[6]

For this age and all ages, parents should be careful not to create for their children false connections to the past. Well intended over-exuberance by the adoptive parents on behalf of birth parents could lead a child to wonder why the separation occurred in the first place. A child needs to understand clearly from the beginning that birth parents could not parent her at that time in her life. The reasons they could not parent are key to healthy understanding. Help her imagine based on truthful perceptions and assumptions. One of the many benefits of creating and sharing a Lifebook is how it helps cultivate a healthy imagination. On the flip side, one adult adoptee describes having such a limited imagination of her birth parents, birth country, and relinquishment because her adoptive parents did not encourage her to draw healthy pictures in her mind of who they were. This left the child curious and growing up with many unanswered questions.

When a child learns her story she is also better able to verbalize it and explain it to others. Vera Fahlberg suggests that a Lifebook can be a means to helping children develop a "cover story" to share with others. For our family, experience has proven that our children need to know what to say to friends, how to say it, and whether they have to say anything at all. They need our guidance for the occasional questions like, "Why don't you live with your 'real' parents?" or "Are you two brothers?" (Our boys are like apples and oranges when it comes to their looks.) One day the boys' neighborhood buddies even asked us if they could adopt our sons. My boys were very eager to hear our response to that. You have most likely experienced a similar line of questioning as well. Carolyn MacInnes suggests families may want to develop a script for dealing with unwanted and difficult questions.[7] A child should also be given permission to refuse any line of questioning based on its personal nature. This is why it is so important to practice questions and answers at home. An adoptive mom proudly tells how her Korean-born son responded to remarks from another child assuming he was Chinese. He stood confidently with both hands on hips and proudly announced, "I'm not Chinese. I'm Korean!" A child who is prepared is better equipped to answer or not answer questions about private matters.

> If you listen to your children
> while they are young, they will
> learn how to listen to you when
> they are older.

Adolescence

By now an adolescent's Lifebook will take on new meaning and her mind and heart will undergo new understanding. She will arrive at this point bringing with her all that she knows from you — the history of her birth, her adoptive family's security and love, and an identity rooted in God. The Lifebook in her possession is priceless, yet it will now be on her terms when she will seek it out. Our role shifts from that of instructor and trainer to being one of coach and guide[8] as she continues to figure out who she is and how much she wants to know about her birth story. The question of, "Who am I?" is not one we can answer for her.[9] She must piece things together for herself as we walk alongside her with encouragement, understanding, affirmation, and prayer. It is a time when questions are not always asked and a time when answers are not always invited. Yet, it is a time when a child's heart and mind are continuously exploring what was, what is, and what could be.

Adolescents are silently asking many questions, such as "Am I wanted? Do I belong? Do you understand me?" Their vulnerability in working out their identity provides fertile ground for doubt. At this stage parents must be even more creative in reconnecting with their teens. In our culture, there are so many messages that are being sent to our children—many often telling them that who they are is not okay. Adolescence is truly a time of confusion and awakening. Parents have the opportunity to affirm and guide their children during this vulnerable stage. (For more resources on connecting with your teen see the Resources page in the back of this book.)

Additional timing tips

While a Lifebook is for all ages, certain information contained in a Lifebook is not always appropriate depending on the age. We like to use the movie rating system of G, PG, and PG13 to put it all in perspective. Our oldest son is fascinated with the back cover of movie jackets right down to the rating system. He knows we only allow movies that are age appropriate, so he is often curious to check out the rating to see what he is missing. Here are a few of his discoveries: peril, mild language, innuendo, violence. And since this book has a G rating we will not take it any further than that. We are not suggesting you put a rating system on your child's Lifebook, but we are suggesting you consider your child's readiness for difficult and potentially confusing information. If something difficult has occurred in his story that you think is beyond a PG13 rating, you may want to seek professional advice before including it in or excluding it from a Lifebook. Cindy Probst, adoption author, advises, "If a particular circumstance is not developmentally appropriate to include, such as conception through violence, you may choose to consult professionals about how and when to share that material with your child." Further, she suggests, "My belief is that a child should not learn of such information for the first time in a Lifebook. Such circumstances might be implied in one's Lifebook in order to keep the Lifebook truthful and to generate discussion."[10] We agree!

When it comes to sharing difficult information, authors Betsy Keefer and Jayne Schooler offer this important advice: "The child is able to understand his story in layers. What he is told at age three may be a simplified version of reality, with more information supplied when he is better able to understand. The child receives another layer of understanding as he matures, and so on until the child has all the information the parent has."[11]

Telling stories in layers has served our family well. However it made preparing a Lifebook a bit tricky. Does one make several different Lifebooks suited for each child's developmental stage? Seems rational for some, but for our family the time commitment involved in such a task proved unreasonable. Therefore, what we found best for our family was to write a complete story from start to finish and relate it, or tell it, in layers. However, we will leave it up to you with the following suggestions in mind, to figure out what works best for your family.

Write a complete story

We urge parents not to wait to write, regardless of age or developmental stage. To be the storyteller is to be prepared. It is important to process and believe your child's story before explaining it to him. You cannot possibly do this trying to recall bits and pieces while in the midst of an emotional blur. Ideally, gather, research, evaluate, process, write, and pray while information, memories, and thoughts are fresh and new.

Pick and choose

Select those parts of his story you will verbally share based on his ability to understand. Remember, this is just the first layer necessary to build a foundation of understanding and openness. For younger children, birth parent and separation details seem to present the greatest opportunity for confusion. This is when some parents opt to create a "toddler book" as a way to ease into their child's story by omitting specific relinquishment details. Another way is to create a cover story that is age appropriate to address these areas. "The cover story is a shortened, not-too revealing version of the truth."[12]

Create privacy

Insert blank pages over delicate information you plan to save for the future. We selected keepsake albums from the local scrapbook store that came with page protectors. Page protectors serve several purposes. They protect the Lifebook pages from little gooey hands, they protect delicate information for the future, and they place a privacy shield over personal information when needed.

Use discretion	When adding potentially confusing photos, such as photos of birth parents, use your discretion, but we suggest that you do not add them earlier than school age. This suggestion applies for children who have not known or have a relationship with birth parents, birth relation, or birth siblings.
Add artwork	Encourage your child's imagination through art. For example, a self-portrait can fill a space where a photo does not exist to create a colorful addition that will later be looked back on with joy. Encourage portraits of birth parents too. Art in a Lifebook can generate healthy conversations.
Find or imagine similarities	List, together with your child, things he may share in common with his birth family.
Discover heritage	Encourage your child to discover his birth heritage and culture.
Add letters	Include letters from any important people that would be helpful.
Go on field trips	Visit the hospital where he was born, former school he attended, or other significant locations. You never know what value a child places on different places or things.
Add faith messages	Include written prayers, Scripture, and perhaps personal poems. When faith messages are included they give evidence of God's glory and they display his faithfulness and provision.

Remember, children can't "unthink" their beginnings. As often as we have heard from adoptive parents that their children have, "put it in the past," or "it is behind her," they have not. The purpose of this chapter is to increase your awareness and understanding of how a child processes her story and what an important role you play in how you reveal her story. We hope you have discovered that your child's story will unfold throughout her life and take on new meaning as she continues to grow. Your role as storyteller is key in helping her to unlock a healthy understanding of herself. May your adopted child experience the emotional freedom of knowing her birth history and the positive effect that embracing her beginning can have on her entire life.

HOMEWORK

ready to hear	Spend some time reflecting on your child's ability to understand and process information. What development stage is your child in? What information is he/she ready to hear? How will you tell him/her?
spend time	Spend some quiet time considering how you will approach your child's Lifebook, knowing how age and developmental stage fit in.

The truest test for any prayer is
always the heart. What is our
intention?[1]

— HEATHER HARPHAM KOPP

CHAPTER 4

A Lifebook and Prayer

God's invitation

We prayed that God would make adoption a part of our lives, and one by one our three children came to us over the years, through the miracle of adoption. We are not sure how God works that out, but he often reveals himself in surprising ways, and there are many things we cannot explain lest we minimize his very self. Whether he asked us to adopt or we asked him if we could becomes unimportant. What matters is that the God of the known universe and beyond invites us to respond to many needs … adoption being one. When we accept the invitation or ask to be invited, the miracle unfolds.

Questions, fears, and the unknown

My husband and I agree there were many unknowns along the way and plenty to worry about when we started the process to adopt our first son. Not knowing what was in store for us, we began our adoption journey with simple prayers of concerns we could wrap our minds around at that point in the process. We first prayed for safety — for our own and for our child who was waiting for us somewhere in an unfamiliar part of the world. We would eventually discover that we would travel halfway around the world to a place that was just waking up from years of Communist rule.

Our prayers began to change as God's plan unfolded. They shifted to issues like, "Will you please show me what it takes to be a mom?" and "Who is this little stranger you have sent to join our lives forever?" Then the unknown shifted to fear when the potential for health concerns like Fetal Alcohol Syndrome, encephalopathy, and others barely pronounceable entered in. Our prayers again changed. Facing all this and undoubtedly more, we chose to accept the unknown and acknowledge our fears. We were not turning back. We chose to trust that God was working out the details that were out of our control. He was leading us to our child—a child we believe was meant for us since the beginning of time.

Despite our fears, unanswerable questions, and all the unknowns that stretched us like only adoption can, a baby boy joined our family. Our hearts sang! Scripture beautifully reminds us to "Sing to him, sing praise to him; tell of all his wonderful acts" (Ps 105:2). The hand of God had created a new family.

Over and over again, a similar story of adoption is told by parents everywhere. Ours is not unique. But what stands out is the realization that something powerful is going on when so many adoptive families enter into and become a part of the remarkable way God uses adoption. We believe our first priority then should be to humbly accept God's calling and discover all that he has for us and our children.

Moving forward with God

It took an anniversary trip to Mexico with my husband (without kids), and the solitude found there to reflect more fully on the lives of our children. Let's face it, being in the day-to-day chaos of parenting had kept us in the present, and we were often more reactive rather than proactive in our prayer life. Three small children all close in age is enough to keep parents fully occupied until they collapse in bed each night. In the peace and quiet of our tropical beachside resort, I sensed a stirring in my heart. I felt not only a desire but a *need* to change the way I prayed for our children. Their past, present, and future were all a part of them and who they would become, and yet my prayers for them were only based on the present. I had not intentionally ignored their past nor had I intentionally not considered their future, it just had not dawned on me until I sat quietly with the Lord. He showed me what was missing from my prayers. As I listened, God stirred the pot to bubbling over. My heart was open to praying differently, so I began writing a list. It was a scramble of notes that ignited peace and joy and a sense of urgency all at the same time. God was showing me both how to embrace our children's birth stories and how to pray for each of them uniquely because of their stories. For the first time, I began to realize that our children faced a loss that would challenge their very perception of who God created them to be—that their relinquishment was and is a permanent part of their big picture, and that I could not predict if its impact would be minimal or substantial. Of this I am sure, God was showing me all of this for a reason. He was urging me to entrust them to him and inviting me to partner with him through prayer.

Counting on us

Our children are most likely counting on us to discover their story, to know their story, to pray for their hearts, to hear them, to affirm them, to protect them, to guide them, and to listen for a stirring from God. They may want us to remember their past with them and to imagine their future with them. We get to tell them how special they are and who God created them to be. What an opportunity! In the midst of our busy lives, we urge you to remember that one of our most important jobs as parents is to show them the kind of love that God lavishes on us. God invites us to join him as we step into the profound responsibility of parenting.

A Lifebook and prayer

Because writing a Lifebook will potentially open a child's mind to questions, concerns, fears, and grief, parents' prayers play an important role. We believe a Lifebook, for lack of better words, is a "do-it-yourself counseling tool" that God longs to be a part of. Saturating the past, present, and future with prayers for our children connects them to the healing power of God and his abundant wisdom and divine guidance. And, it changes us as parents. We are convinced a Lifebook and prayer belong together.

In her book *The Power of a Praying Parent*, author Stormie Omartian strongly encourages parents that "It's not enough to pray only for the concerns of the moment; we need to pray for the future and we need to pray against the effects of past events."[2]

Why should we pray?

I was listening to the heart of my six-year-old one day as he gave this description of what adoption means to him. It surprised me to hear the depth of understanding in his words. "Adoption is good and bad," he said. "Bad that you are born and you grow up and have to be adopted. Good that you get to go into a new family. Birth parents are your real parents and adoptive parents are your second real family." Wow, was I given a glimpse into our son's heart and reason to pray in a new way! The reality is our children have been exposed to adoption conversations and their Lifebooks for a while now, but this type of response at such a young age still surprises me. I often think this is the stuff that shows up during the tumultuous teen years. So I am reminded that children, regardless of age, are processing their relinquishment and adoption whether they are talking about it or not. The good news is that a Lifebook helps open the window of your child's heart — the very place you want to be and the very place God desires to be. When you go there, remember how God longs to be a part of this journey too. This is not a journey God wants us to walk alone. We are invited to partner with him along the way. It is in sitting in his presence, talking with him and listening to his voice where we come to know his heart. His timeless counsel will guide you as you sensitively and compassionately engage your child in adoption conversations.

> To pray unceasingly is to channel our thoughts out of their fearful isolation into a fearless conversation with God.[3]
>
> — HENRI NOUWEN

Below are some guidelines to use as you prepare for and enter into adoption conversations.

Be slow to speak	"The words of the reckless pierce like swords, but the tongue of the wise brings healing" (Prov. 12:18).
Be quick to listen	"Everyone should be quick to listen ..." (James 1:19).
Be understanding	"Someone's thoughts may be as deep as the ocean, but if you are smart, you will discover them" (Prov. 20:5 CEV).

Pray in the moment

Don't wait until the next time you find a quiet moment to pray, because that is a rarity.

"This is the confidence we have in approaching God: that if we ask anything according to his will, he hears us" (1 John 5:14).

For the record, we want to send the message to you that prayer is not a form of rescue, but rather an invitation to take your questions and feelings to God and allow his wisdom and heart to speak to you. Prayer is a vital addition to what you are already doing. If you have not been praying for your child, you can begin today. Nancy Guthrie, in her article *Prayers That Move the Heart of God*, writes, "When our prayers move from the superficial to the significant, we invite God to do no less than a deep, transforming, igniting work in our life and in the lives of those for whom we're praying."[4]

The list

The prayer list that I started in Mexico grew as a result of an informal prayer survey we conducted while writing this book. We wanted to find out what prayer concerns and praises were on the hearts of other adoptive parents, and did they come through! There were many, and we have dispersed some in the rest of this book with the greatest concentration listed below. Use them to guide you in your conversations with God.

Parents' prayer for child

To know he/she is loved.

To know he/she belongs.

To feel safe and have a sense of security.

To have a healthy self-esteem and identity.

To openly share his/her needs, concerns, and questions.

To feel understood.

To seek God's heart.

To deepen his/her relationship with God.

To know and seek God's purpose for his/her life.

To develop healthy relationships with others.

To embrace his/her story.

To honor his/her birth parents.

To be able one day to forgive the people in his/her life that could not stay with them.

To grieve his/her loss in a healthy way.

To receive healing from any brokenness caused by his/her relinquishment.

To know the gifts and talents he/she brings to this world are needed.

To know how he/she uniquely displays God's image.

To know who God created him/her to be.

To live the way God created him/her to live.

To know he/she is valuable.

To see God's essential role in all of who he/she is.

Creating empathy

To help you discover more of your child's specific prayer needs, it would be beneficial for you as a parent to revisit your own childhood and think about what you needed and/or longed for as you experienced life. This creates empathy and allows you to personally connect more with your child's heart and needs. For example, I needed to hear that my parents loved me. So, now I pray that the messages I send through my words and actions will tell my children how much I love them.

On the next page are helpful suggestions we, as parents, can pray for ourselves.

Parents' prayer

To create a safe and open environment for adoption talk.

To be sensitive and aware that our child is, or may one day be, grieving his/her relinquishment and be able to enter into that process.

To be supportive and nonjudgmental of birth parents or birth parent choices.

To be compassionate and truthful in telling our child his/her birth history.

To face and release any fears and build the courage to tell our child any painful truths.

To recognize our child's strengths, gifts, and talents and build on them.

To call out and encourage our child's unique identity.

To help us understand how our child was affected by his/her relinquishment and know that he/she may have unresolved grief issues.

To use us in a powerful way to be our child's safe haven if or when things become confusing.

To guide our child with wisdom, discernment, compassion, and humility.

To clearly hear, know, and believe our child's heart.

To cultivate a healthy parenting style to meet our child's specific needs.

To hear and be sensitive to God's direction and instruction.

To be aware of any personal issues that may hinder healthy parenting.

To receive God's grace when we make mistakes.

To ask God to create a spirit of unity in our parenting.

Just as our children need lifting up to the Lord—so do parents. Parenting, we believe, is a responsibility and gift given to us by God. Have you ever asked God to work in you and through you? Do you believe he can?

HOMEWORK

prayer list

Think of your child's past, present, and future as you consider a prayer list for him/her and perhaps a prayer journal for you. Carve out quite moments as you work through the process of making your child's Lifebook and consider his/her heart and your own. Ask God to stir in you a desire to pray for your son or daughter in a very specific way. Use the lists we have provided as your guide. Note: As your child grows, what will your list look like? How will it change? How will your prayers change? By keeping a prayer journal you can check back from time to time and see what God is doing in his/her life. You will be amazed at what God reveals to you through these sacred moments of prayer and reflection.

Personal prayer introduction

Our desire is that you will be moved to pray for your child in a renewed, specific, and powerful way, and that the process of preparing a Lifebook will open your eyes and heart to the many areas in your child's life that will need to be saturated in prayer.

In the beginning, we were so amazed when our children came home through adoption that we praised God and thanked God. What parent wouldn't? And then our daily lives took over and we often forgot to include God. We relied on our own human wisdom and strength—something that is all too easy to do. Prayer needs to be an intentional part of our daily life—for us and for our family. Our children, we believe, have been designed by God and are heirs of God (Rom 8:16–17). With that in mind, we have included "Personal prayer" in several places that will help you pray in specific ways for your child. God desires for us to move from thinking and wondering about our children to talking about them, *with* him. Jesus invited us to seek his Father's heart—an invitation echoed by James when he wrote,

> "Come near to God and he will come near to you."

> — JAMES 4:8

Personal prayer

LORD, we don't know what **[insert child's name]**'s future holds, but you do. We have so many hopes and dreams for her, but she is not our creation, she is yours. When we think of how much life she has ahead of her and all the things that are unknown, we know now that we need your help and need to partner with you, because your wisdom and guidance reveal what is right and good. Increase our faith to believe you are able to do immeasurably more than we can possibly imagine. Show us how to pray for her. Place her needs on our heart. (*This is a good time to personalize this prayer for your child further by referring to the specific needs and concerns from lists on previous pages.*) We do not want **[child's name]** to miss out on the purpose and plan you have intended for her. Secure her future. Show your favor upon her. We pray for your protection over her mind and heart. Now God, we ask that you make us aware of our own needs as a parent. (*This is where you are invited to personalize the prayer for you by referring to the lists on previous pages.*) We need to slow down and listen to the Holy Spirit's prompting in our lives and that of our child's. We choose to give our child to you. Amen.

PART II

Discovering My Child's Story

What we have to learn to do, we
learn by doing.

—ARISTOTLE

CHAPTER 5

Where Do We Begin?

Laurel's story

I cannot remember what we ordered that night at the restaurant. Our conversation quickly consumed us as we spoke of her two little girls adopted from China. Memories of each adoption trip were still so fresh. Talking about Lifebooks was the furthest thing from her mind. But, she was my friend and she allowed me to quiz her intently regarding the tragic abandonment of both her girls, sadly the story of most little girls adopted from China. With her eyes welling up with tears, we searched through documents looking for clues to their past when she abruptly said to me "I have nothing! A Lifebook doesn't make sense under these circumstances." It was my turn to release the tears. I thought of my own three children adopted from Russia. At least I had details, but they were sketchy at best.

I spent the next two hours convincing my friend Laurel that she *did* have enough information to develop a story for her girls. And what she did not have, she would have to work to find. It would require researching her girls' birth country. She would have to search the web to find other adoptive families through chat rooms with daughters from the same region of China or the same orphanage who could answer questions. She would have to recall the memories of their two adoption trips, using her senses to remember sights, sounds, smells, and tastes. She would also need to learn about and understand the motivation behind abandonment of baby girls in China. She would need to learn how to frame difficult information and do it in an age-appropriate way.

She would have to bring honor to the birth parents for her children's sake, making assumptions about their character in light of having no information about them. I left Laurel that night with much to think about. Deep inside I knew the journey ahead of her would take time and effort, but the potential rewards for her, her husband, and their daughters would be significant.

Laurel's story is not uncommon. Adoptive parents are often willing and wanting to discover their child's story but do not know where to begin. It is tough to begin when many adoptions are closed, or begin in abandonment as in Laurel's story. But starting is just what we need to do. Here is why: Families with little or sketchy information, like my friend in the story, more than ever need to create something tangible, truthful, huggable, and available for their children, so the story feels more real and so the miles and years that span the separation from their birth origin do not diminish the importance of their beginning. For families fortunate enough to have a lot of information, it is about making sense of it all in an organized, loving, and sensitive way. So whether your child is four, fourteen, or twenty-four, she has a Lifebook—a permanent piece of her past that can be carried with her throughout her life.

Some may question, "Are we making a mountain out of a molehill?" "Are we opening a can of worms and causing unnecessary tension and stress in our lives, our child's life, or in our parent/child relationship?" Let us assure you that making and sharing a Lifebook for and with your child is exactly the opposite. It is the most nonthreatening thing you can present to your child. It is a gift because it is a part of her lifestory.

Here is one example why a Lifebook is beneficial. My oldest son who, at the time, was seven years old, rarely showed much interest in his birth story and he certainly shied away from any talk of his birthmother. It was, and still is, the stage he is in. But I knew it was important to bring the topic up from time to time and test the waters. If I asked him whether he wondered about his birthmother he would usually say, "No." But, if I changed up the question and asked if he would like to look at his Lifebook, he almost always said, "Yes." You see, it is all about how I approached his story. He seems much less intimidated by his Lifebook than by my specific questions. When I proactively offer him birth information it seems to bring up mixed emotions and confusion and he often shuts down. Offering him his Lifebook is less threatening and allows him to explore the areas he is most interested in. For example, all our children love to hear about the time zone difference between the United States and Russia. They giggle when they imagine the people in Russia sleeping while we are awake. Something as simple as this can get healthy adoption conversations going. Because our children are different ages, they are fascinated with different areas of their books. We get a window into what they are most interested in with the questions that naturally surface. We love our Lifebooks because they are good conversation starters. This takes the pressure off us. For our family, it is just easier for us to say, "Let's look at your Lifebook." It is amazing what conversations follow.

Back to Laurel's story

Laurel had a lot of questions for me that night, but she also had concerns. "How do I do this thing right?" (It was still a "thing" and not a passion, yet.) "Where will I find the time?" (She was a busy mom with plenty of priorities.) "What if I don't do it?" (Would she be missing an opportunity of a lifetime?) Let's take a closer look at these questions.

How do I do this right?

There is no right or wrong way to make a Lifebook. Let's put that concern to rest right now. If you have never seen a Lifebook before it can be hard to visualize what one might look like. In Part III of this book, you will find examples from actual Lifebook pages to help you visualize your own. There are many examples given as a springboard for your own creativity. Go ahead, take a look. Remember, a Lifebook is a story — a book that displays pictures, documents, stories, and information about your child's life prior to adoption. You can create your own unique format and style.

Where will I find the time?

Lack of time has the greatest potential for being a showstopper. Lack of time, not desire, was reported by parents to be the number-one obstacle to getting started on a Lifebook. Let's face it, given how families are spread so thin these days, finding the time can be a challenge, and believe me, I am sensitive to this. I have three young children and have faced this challenge myself. It was one of the many motivations for writing this book. When making a Lifebook, keep things simple and make the most of your time. It is not about how much you can put in a Lifebook, but rather what you put in it. Our hope is that what you create comes out of your heart and that the pieces you include are important for your child to know about her story.

What if I don't do it?

Your child's story needs to come from you. If you wait too long to tell her, someone else may come along and do the job for you — perhaps an older sibling, a cousin, or a school friend — all have the potential to share inaccurate information or present it in an insensitive way. When she sees you working on it, your child will discover you are making a Lifebook for her, which will send the message that her adoption and adoption talk are okay. Chances are she may even want to work alongside you.

Waiting too long can also produce unnecessary anxiety. The process of preparing a Lifebook is just as important as the outcome. Talking to a child about her birth details, separation from her birth family, abandonment, and more may leave a parent feeling anxious if unprepared. This process will help uncover any hidden emotions that you may need to confront, and there is value in practicing the story, too.

Finally, creating a Lifebook is a chance to bless your child. Adopted children need to know their birth stories. Parents need to tell. If you put off this important privilege, you could miss a chance to share God's heart *for* and *in* her story and his redemptive work in her life.

What about writing the story?

At first glance it may appear you do not have enough information, as Laurel believed, to even attempt to write a story. In the following chapters you will discover questionnaires that will help you discover the details you need to write your child's story. When I began working on my children's books, I had a hard time both visualizing what a Lifebook could be and what to write about. In response to my challenges in getting started, I developed (with the help of two other adoptive moms) extensive questionnaires that gave us a logical format to follow. I then started sharing them with other adoptive parents and began offering Lifebook workshops. Hundreds of parents attended these workshops seeking direction and encouragement. It was affirming to see how valuable our resources were to these parents, thus confirming their value to us and now to you.

A marathon and not a sprint

It comes as no surprise that this project is not a sprint but rather a marathon, a walk or run type marathon that allows you to go at your own pace. Like a breast cancer walk, you participate because of the passion in your heart for the cause. As you mentally and emotionally prepare to begin, consider these important suggestions.

Suggestion 1	**Develop a vision** for this Lifebook cause. Take some time to think through why you would make a Lifebook for your child. Allow the energy and passion to develop. Do this because you are compelled to do it, not because you "have to" do it.
Suggestion 2	**Devise a strategy** like most marathon participants do. Start with the exercises (homework) found in this book. You may even want to set small goals to accomplish. Take the time to understand and embrace the idea of a Lifebook.
Suggestion 3	**Drop whatever is necessary** to make this Lifebook a priority. You may need to make temporary changes in your schedule that will allow you the adequate time to create a Lifebook. Getting rid of outside distractions will allow you to stay focused.
Suggestion 4	**Consider finding a marathon partner** who is interested in creating a Lifebook, too. This will give both of you an accountability partner and someone who is willing to support and encourage you to set aside time and stick to your commitment.
Suggestion 5	**Sponsor someone who can run in your place.** Meaning, if you really cannot find the time but still have the desire to make a Lifebook for your child, find someone you know and trust to do it for you. This is not uncommon. I have written Lifebooks for my friends' children. I have found it much easier to write someone else's story with the emotional component gone than writing for my own children. A simple interview with one or

Suggestion 6

both parents to go over details and sort through documents can set a project quickly in motion.

Consider your child's age and current needs. If your child is school age and asking questions about her relinquishment, you may feel like you are playing catch-up. Ask yourself, "What does she need to know now?" and focus on sharing that first. For example, it would be okay to start your research with the separation story or how to honor your child's birth parents as a short term solution. Ideally we recommend you start from the beginning of your child's story so that you can fully prepare to become the storyteller. However, it may be necessary for you to choose to start with only a few questionnaires that meet your immediate needs.

Tips for waiting families

Create a Lifebook file now while you wait for your child to come home, with the intent of keeping Lifebook material separate from other adoption information. Distinguishing between the details now will better prepare you for the work ahead.

Keep a daily journal and watch God work as your adoption process unfolds.

Begin praying and asking God to reveal to you what is important to capture about your child's life. Allow your eyes and ears to be "open" to what might be important parts of your child's story before adoption.

Now go get those folders and boxes and gather what pre-adoption data you already have about your child and let's get started.

HOMEWORK

Getting organized

As you have just discovered, there are several keys to getting started and staying on course to complete your child's Lifebook. Now it is time to consider what format you will choose to tell your child's story. Will you make a scrapbook by hand, design an online storybook, or simply write a journal? How will you get organized?

decide

Decide on a size for your Lifebook. Make a visit to your local scrapbook store or go online and become acquainted with all of the many possibilities for the size of your book. We recommend you choose a book that will hold fifteen or more pages and is 8" x 8" or larger. You will also find color-coordinated papers and other themed items that may fit into your plan. Since scrapbooking (scrapping) is so popular now, it fits perfectly with the Lifebook concept. Journaling only? Select a journal that is keepsake quality that may also have pockets for holding cherished items such as letters, newspaper clippings, and photos.

organize

Organize Lifebook information. Sort through adoption files, selecting only those documents and photos relevant for this project. Search with help from the checklist found on the next page. The checklist will help you make good choices for your book. Copy or scan originals and return originals to a safe place. Do not use originals since they can rarely be replaced. Ideally, purchase an inexpensive folder with clear, top loading pockets. Label each pocket according to the checklist on this page. Organize your photos and documents accordingly.

internet Investigate the Internet and find out what is available for your project that you can download such as supporting graphics like flags, maps, cultural and historical information from your child's country, state, or city. This is a great place for waiting parents to start while anticipating their child's arrival.

find a partner Find an accountability partner. We cannot stress enough how helpful it is to find another adoptive parent you can trust who will help hold you accountable and will work on your Lifebook with you. Busy parents will find it much easier to set aside time if they have each other to encourage.

Checklist of pre-adoption photos and documents

- ❑ All child photos organized by age
- ❑ All photos of birth hospital, foster care home, orphanage, finding location
- ❑ All photos of orphanage caregivers
- ❑ Birth certificate and or other important documents
- ❑ Birth parents' photos and notes (reserve for older children)
- ❑ Foster family photos and notes
- ❑ Birth sibling photos
- ❑ Friends prior to adoption
- ❑ School, pets, special occasion photos
- ❑ Birth country, state and city photos, maps, and flags
- ❑ Photos of adopted friends pre- and post-adoption
- ❑ Most current photos of your family
- ❑ Most current photos of your child

CHAPTER 6

Imagine

Born into less-than-ideal circumstances

There is a story of a child who was rarely held for the first several critical months of her life.

There is a story of a child whose young birthmother gave birth, left the hospital without her newborn, was tracked down by government authorities and forced to parent for a year only to abandon her child again, for a second time.

There is a story of a child whose teen birth parents were not ready to parent him at that time in their lives.

There is a story of a child who lived his first four years of life in an orphanage. He was both mentally and physically delayed.

There is a story of a child who was placed near a dumpster by her drug-addicted birthmother.

There is a story of a child who was placed on the steps of a police station. After being quickly discovered, she was taken to an overcrowded orphanage to share a crib with another orphaned baby.

Imagining more

These stories were gathered from adoptive parents who were willing to share them with us. They are poignant reminders of the less than ideal circumstances many relinquished children start life with. When we hear these types of stories, we find two things are often missing. Rarely do we hear the side of the story that reveals the child, and more often than not, when we hear these types of stories, they are quickly followed by comments like, "This is all we know."

This is all we know. *Hmm.* Let's think about why this happens. Typically, a child's separation story is the first story told to prospective parents by adoption coordinators while waiting, maybe months or years, for their child to be ready to adopt. Unfortunately, there is plenty of time to dwell on it and, we think it is safe to say, it is also the first story most prospective parents want to know. For example, I remember when my husband and I sat across the desk from our adoption coordinator, asking what happened. "Why is he (our future son) available?" "What happened to him after his birthmother left the hospital?" The answers to these and other questions became imprinted on our minds because, for a while, this was all we knew while we waited. No wonder *this* is often the only part of the story we are so well rehearsed in and the one that rolls off our tongues first before anything else, especially when talking with other adoptive parents. No wonder parents often fear revealing what they know when they believe there is not much more they can say. The scale seems tipped in one direction; it seems out of balance somehow. We do not want to minimize the importance of these first pieces of information, because when parents wait for a child, any news is cherished. But, they do need to balance that scale the best they can. It is important that adoptive parents have more information. So, pause for a moment, take a deep breath, and think of all the blessings you may have overlooked that reveal the child, *your* child.

One of the benefits for us is getting to watch parents become visibly relieved when we begin to imagine together the possibilities that can fill in the missing days, weeks, months, or years of their child's life prior to joining their family. We begin by imagining their child without the relinquishment story attached, temporarily separating that story so we can see what else is there. And what do we see? A good baby (a *must* to say in any Lifebook)! Born with wispy, strawberry-blond hair. We see a perfect nose. And what about those toes? She was not randomly put together by careless chance, was she? Every part of her is priceless and, in our Creator's eyes, she is a princess with an eternal heritage to claim. What about her nature? Can we see her personality, or her instinct to fight through sadness, sickness, or fear? Did she cry a lot to give her caregiver a reason to hold her? Or, did she know what she wanted and how to get it? Much of this is right before your eyes and stirring in your heart when you look at your child today. The point is that parents need to discover the details of their child's beginning and burst with the emotion that tells the world this baby was born. Claim that excitement even if you were not there at her birth. The angels did! The angels praised God when a certain young King was born in less than perfect circumstances to a teenage girl in a common stable 2000 years or so ago. They danced and sang for the new life God had brought forth (Heb 1:6).

Not wanting to overlook the blessing of our daughter's birth, I began her Lifebook with a simple poem I wrote so that she could understand the beauty of her birth and life at her young age.

> *When babies are born around the world,*
> *Angels sing and dance and twirl.*
> *A celebration for all of heaven to see,*
> *God made it happen, you were meant to be.*

Then we wrote to our little girl about her life in Russia as a baby before we adopted her. "You were bundled cozy tight as is the tradition in Russia. You kept busy sleeping and eating, too, just like all new babies do. As you grew each day you did wonderful things — like roll over, hold your head high, and crawl." The poem then continued:

> *Watching over close and near,*
> *Angels whisper in your ear,*
> *"Your Heavenly Father is close at hand,*
> *He knows your needs, He has a plan."*

Another family began their daughter's book with a blessing from Scripture, "Children are a heritage from the Lord" (Ps 127:3). With the help of a computer scrapbook program the verse was displayed like a beautiful rainbow on the first page of her Lifebook. A poem then followed underneath it.

> *Imagine*
> *Puts both hands on bottle*
> *Likes to see it*
> *Sleeps lying on her back*
> *Turns her head when called by name*
> *Laughs aloud*
> *Babbles well*
> *Reaches*
> *Cries*
> *Is not shy*
> *A cute and lovable baby girl*

What is so wonderful about this example is that, except for the word "Imagine," all of the other words in this poem were taken from this child's medical report, which included basic observations by the doctor and caregiver. You can do this, too! Most of this is what all babies do. These are the special and vital pieces available to parents if they only look. These are the special moments that can be captured in a Lifebook to help a child realize his worth even as a baby born in less than ideal circumstances.

A toddler's story

Our first introduction to our second son, Nickolai, came from a video we received from another family that had visited the baby home in Russia where our son was living. What we saw was a shy, sleepy, cranky, maybe even sick, 20-month-old precious little boy having a bad day. This was our second adoption, and we were not fazed at all by what we saw. Rather, we liked how he was standoffish and put off by the video camera. His attitude revealed his mind was working just fine and it was telling him something is not right. This pouty-faced little boy was not just lying around, nor was he posed for an adoption magazine photo shoot. He was showing his true colors.

When we arrived at the orphanage in the small Russian town to meet our son, of course we wanted to see him right away. We anticipated he would be uncomfortable with strangers, so we asked if he could stay with his small group and we would slowly move towards him. Bubbles, suckers, and an hour of play later, Nickolai maintained his distance with a healthy suspicion. Once we spotted him running over to his caregiver to wrap his arms around her apron-covered legs as if running to his mother. She exchanged the hugs with some tender cuddles and he was refueled and ready to play some more. What an important clue — that he knew love, could receive love, and could give love. Then, the moment we had waited for came. He climbed on his new daddy's lap and warmed right up in his arms.

These memories of meeting our second son were ours to treasure. However, almost two years of Nickolai's life went by without us. From what we could see, he had accomplished a lot. He had learned to roll over, crawl, walk, feed himself, go potty independently, and respond well to instructions. He was impressively organized, tidy, and could even dress himself. Even though we never saw him reach these important milestones, he was reaching them—and exceeding them—without us. Meeting his developmental milestones told us a lot, and so did the clues we gathered as we watched him in his Russian baby home that day. He was healthy, loving, and living in a caring environment. The point is, we began thinking of his story in terms of him, not his relinquishment, and it freed us up to imagine that important part of his life.

One video, two priceless baby photos, a medical report, and our memories may have been all we had, but these proved to be almost all we needed to get started on Nickolai's Lifebook. We also consulted a trusted parenting resource, *The Complete Book of Baby & Child Care* from Focus on the Family.[1] Of course any similar resource will do. This book gave us a complete tour of a child's development from conception through infancy and all the way through to adolescence. We found a wealth of information that filled in the missing two years of Nickolai's development. So we started there. We began painting a picture of what this little guy had been up to for the past two years. In one sense we were stating the obvious, what most children do, but to our child we were showing him a precious piece of his story that many adoptive parents overlook or consider unimportant. If parents do not talk about their child's birth and life prior to adoption, it could be perceived by the child as a secret. Children often perceive secrets as bad and, if the secrets are about them, they may assume *they* are bad, too.[2]

> Talking about birth and
> pre-adoption years is the first
> step in verifying a child's belief
> that he was a good baby or
> correcting erroneous beliefs that
> he was not good.

Ask yourself, "What is my child looking for in his birth story that now only I can show him?" "What blessings, clues, and evidence can I discover that will help him feel valuable?"

Here are a few items that are worth looking for in addition to what we have already shared.

Signs of love, care, and value

Signs of God's protection and plan

Signs of being a good baby, being wanted and created for a purpose

Signs of birth parent intentions (explored more in chapter 8)

Signs of being safe or made safe

Signs of trust or broken trust

Signs of healthy, physical development or not

Signs of personality and temperament

Without a doubt, we knew our children would also be interested in facts and data that would lead them to a greater awareness and understanding of their stories: interesting things about their birth, their personality as a baby, whether or not they sucked a thumb or fingers. Practical things like who took care of them before they were adopted, how long they were there (foster care, orphanage, or first home) and whether they were healthy, safe, sick, happy, or sad. They may want to know what their caregivers or foster parents were like and whether they missed them. Eventually they will begin asking questions and will want to know why they were adopted. These are all interesting and important pieces of your child's beginning. As the storyteller, having already imagined and explored the answers to these questions and more will someday be a gift to them.

Connect the dots

Our children love to play Connect the Dots, where a picture comes alive as you move a crayon from the first letter in the alphabet forward, or from one number to the next. But, when they were too young to know where to start, our children just connected the dots in their own way. Often the pictures were distorted, but they were too young to notice, and we were too kind to let them know. With a little guidance, they started getting good at connecting the dots and the pictures became what they were intended to be. As adopted children grow, they connect the dots about their birth story whether we are guiding them or not. Imagine if we guide them in an age-appropriate way and are sensitive to their developmental stages. The picture they create will become more fully developed and less distorted. Otherwise, we leave connecting the dots to them and who knows what picture will appear.

Help is on the way

The next part of this chapter is an introduction to the first in a series of questionnaires that offer the help you need for what we have discussed so far. It will be an exploration in going beyond the given in an attempt to reveal your child. It will be a fill-in-the-blank exercise where you can provide answers and offer safe assumptions by imagining more than just the relinquishment story. The first questionnaire is an important starting point because you will begin developing the opening story of your child's Lifebook. Consider this: Depending on the age of your child prior to joining your family, we believe you should minimally be able to recapture glimpses of his birth, infancy, and toddler stages. As suggested earlier, it helps to review a baby book that describes developmental milestones for each of these stages. In most cases while you were not there to witness special events like rolling over, cutting teeth, or walking, you get to imagine and confirm it all now by relying on what most babies do. Your child will be thrilled to hear about his infancy even if it is only in general terms. So, do not get caught up on dates.

Finally, help shape your child's view of himself by telling him how God sees him. Remember to insert God's present and heart in the story with Scripture. In addition to the questionnaires, you will discover a section called, "Claim it" loaded with supporting Scripture specifically selected for you to prayerfully consider, claim, share with your child, and use for the pages of his book. Each verse you choose is a gentle reminder to your child of God's love for him.

We have also collected prayers contributed by many adoptive parents and we encourage you to begin praying for your child's past, present, and future. We introduced specific adoption prayer items earlier in chapter 4. When we willingly lean on God through prayer, and ask him to reveal our child's needs with clarity and vision, we can trust he will lay those needs on our hearts and minds. Prayer is one way we can stay connected to God throughout this process.

The Bible seems to always be
saying that this journey is indeed
a journey, a journey always
initiated and concluded by God,
and a journey of transformation
much more than mere education
about anything.[3]

— RICHARD ROHR

Important guidelines

We do not expect you to have all the answers to the following questions. We recognize you may just have a few. Do what you can with what you have and follow the suggestions on page 73 along with these last few important guidelines.

Make assumptions and guesses

As you respond to as many questions as you can, we encourage you to make safe assumptions or best guesses where there is not enough information, guided by the truth in your child's story. Author Beth O'Malley introduced this approach in her book, *Lifebooks: Creating a Treasure for the Adopted Child,* to help adoptive parents expand the amount of information they have when it seems there is not enough. Safe assumptions that do not mislead can increase the level of fullness to a story with few details. Should you choose to make safe assumptions, we caution you, as discussed in an earlier chapter, not to create any unrealistic or false connections to the past that could leave an adopted child longing for someone or something that is just not there. Remember, adopted children need to understand why as an infant, baby, toddler, or older child they were separated from their birth parents and the significance of that separation.

It's okay to not know	It is okay and important to write, "We do not know," for questions you cannot answer. You will return to these responses later as you write and use these very words to fill in for missing information. Telling your child you do not know something is honest and also a form of information. Omitting information leaves the window of fantasy cracked open.
Determine writing style	Determine your writing style. Once you have completed the questionnaire, consider how you will write the information in the pages of the book. Some parents have written sentences with bullet points, others write captions under photos or graphics. Some include poems or write a story that begins with "Once upon a time." (See chapter 10.) Again, there are many ways to display the information.

May you see your child's beginning in a new way, and may the God who sees guide you to that truth.

HOMEWORK

discover your child

Questionnaire 1 — Imagine

Respond to all questions that are appropriate for your situation remembering to answer, "We do not know," only when necessary. Note: These questionnaires were designed for both international and domestic adoptions, so skip questions that do not apply to your situation. Remember to answer honestly and include both difficult and good information.

1. Child's birth name.
2. Birth name translation.
3. Who named your child at birth?
4. What is the meaning behind her name?
5. Child's adoptive or given name.
6. Interesting story behind her given name?

7. Child's birth date or celebrated date.

8. Day of the week your child was born.

9. Describe the season your child was born.

10. Where was your child born? Placed after birth? Describe the place where your child was found if age appropriate.

11. List baby keepsakes from child's birth country or first set of parents (e.g., blanket, shoes, clothes, notes).

12. Child's birth language.

13. Words your child spoke or understood in birth language.

14. Describe typical "baby things" your child may have been doing even though you did not experience them. Review pediatric milestones from developmental resources.

15. Birth weight or general size (e.g., premature, average, large).

16. Birth length (specific or general).

17. Hair color.

18. Eye color.

19. Location of birthmark(s).

20. Health/development progress.

21. Apgar score and what it meant.

22. Full-term labor or early delivery? Why?

23. Sucked thumb/pacifier/fingers/other?

24. Baby's nature (wiggly, busy, calm, content).

25. Interesting ways baby was held, carried, swaddled.

26. Review medical documents for a general health report or specific key words that best describe your child's health.

27. Describe God's miracle through your child's birth. For example: God's protection during pregnancy and birth, his provision through caregivers, and his plan for adoption. Praise God for your child in written words.

HOMEWORK

Put a checkmark by developmental milestones prior to adoption. Add dates and/or age if you have them or make general assumptions based on pediatric milestones. Keep it simple. Your page layout for this should be creative so that you can proudly display these wonderful firsts. (See Chapter 10.)

baby's firsts

- ❏ 1. Sat unsupported
- ❏ 2. First tooth
- ❏ 3. Smiled
- ❏ 4. Laughed
- ❏ 5. First solid food
- ❏ 6. Responded to name
- ❏ 7. Rolled over
- ❏ 8. Rolled from tummy to back
- ❏ 9. Laid on stomach
- ❏ 10. Responded to name
- ❏ 11. Held head up
- ❏ 12. Cooed
- ❏ 13. Sucked thumb/hand
- ❏ 14. First bottle
- ❏ 15. Slept through night
- ❏ 16. First pulling self up
- ❏ 17. Other

toddler's firsts

- ❏ 1. Talked
- ❏ 2. Fed self
- ❏ 3. Walked
- ❏ 4. Toddler bed
- ❏ 5. Toiletted self
- ❏ 6. Dressed self
- ❏ 7. Other

child's favorites

Children adopted at an older age will need as much of their history filled in that can be shared from documents, previous caregivers, child's memories, or photos.

Activities:

Food:

Toys:

Friends:

Books:

Other:

baby's home and caregivers

For the following questions, use the list of words in the margin below to help you recall the specific details and memories.

The following information will help your child know more about where she was before joining your family. Was she safe? Who cared for her? Was she happy or sad? What did she do? How long was she there? Again, make accurate generalizations if you do not know specifics. Do not forget to answer, "We do not know," if it is true for your situation.

safe

1. Hospital name in English and/or birth country translation of name.

warm

2. Give description of hospital interior/exterior (from photo or memory). For example, was the interior large, small, just right?

smell

condition

3. Where was the hospital located?

size

4. Names of doctors, caregivers, or others responsible for your baby's care.

number of babies

ages

5. What comments/information/letters do you have from
    these caregivers?

cribs

6. How long was your baby there?

location

7. How was your baby treated while in the hospital?

bottles

8. Was your baby happy, sad, content, other?

binkies

9. Baby's routine.

doctors/
nurses

foster care

1. Give description of home exterior/interior (from photo
    or memory).

2. Foster mother/father names.

blankets

3. Foster sibling names.

nursery

4. Significant people in the home worth mentioning.

routine

5. Was it a "traditional" home for the country?

formula

sounds

6. How long was the baby/child there?

colors

teacher

7. Who took the baby/child there?

musical
interests

general
interests

8. What was your impression of these caregivers?
    Attentive, caring, over-extended, committed?

church
activities

9. How was your baby/child treated while in foster care?
    Did your baby/child seem safe, content, healthy, happy,
    sad, isolated, included?

pets

10. Baby's/child's routine.

family
traditions

family
fun times

11. For international adoptions, explain cultural difference
    in child care where it would help a child's understanding.
    For example, "This is the way they do things in your
    birth country."

orphanage

1. Orphanage name. English and/or birth country
    translation of name.

2. Give description of orphanage interior/exterior (from photos or memory). For example, was it large, small, or just right?

3. Where was the orphanage located?

4. Name doctors, directors, caregivers, or others responsible for your baby's/child's care.

5. What comments/information/letters do you have from his or her caregivers?

6. How long was your baby/child there?

7. What was your impression of your baby's/child's caregivers? Attentive, loving, committed, over-extended?

8. How was your baby/child treated while in the orphanage?

9. What was your baby's/child's routine?

10. Describe your impressions of how your baby/child experienced his/her stay there (emotional and physical well being).

11. Explain cultural differences that would lead to your baby's/child's understanding of his/her care while living in the orphanage.

Claim it

Have you ever considered personalizing a promise or a blessing by inserting your child's name in Scripture or prayers? Doing this can be a reminder of what God has done and can still do throughout your child's life. Place it like a banner on the pages of your child's story, so it will be impressed upon your child's heart. Then rely on the Holy Spirit to do the work that will help the seeds you have planted take root.

The Bible verses below have been shared by adoptive parents and were used in their children's Lifebooks. We encourage you to find and claim Scriptures meaningful for your child's Lifebook.

> *"Don't judge each day by the harvest you reap ... but by the seeds you plant."*
>
> ROBERT LOUIS STEVENSON

scripture

But with your own eyes you saw my body being formed. Even before I was born, you had written in your book everything I would do (Ps 139:16 CEV).

I will give them joy for their sorrow (Jer 31:13 NLV).

The Lord said ... "Leave your country ... go to the land I will show you ... I will bless you" (Gn 12:1–2 NLV).

For you are my hiding place; you protect me from trouble. You surround me with songs of victory (Ps 32:7 NLV).

And my God will meet all your needs (Phil 4:19).

I will never leave you. I will never abandon you (Heb 13:5a TEV).

Before I started to put you together in your mother, I knew you (Jer 1:5 NLV).

For you created my inmost being; you knit me together in my mother's womb. I praise you because I am fearfully and wonderfully made, your works are wonderful (Ps 139:13–14).

I will praise you for I am fearfully and wonderfully made (Ps 139:14a NKJV).

I am your Creator. You were in my care even before you were born (Is 44:2a CEV).

I know what I am doing. I have it all planned out—plans to take care of you, not abandon you, plans to give you the future you hope for (Jer 29:11 MSG).

Children are a heritage from the Lord (Ps 127:3).

How wide and long and high and deep is the love of Christ (Eph 3:18).

The Lord is good to all; he has compassion on all he has made (Ps 146:9).

Chosen by God and precious (1 Pt 2:4).

I am a child of God (see Jn 1:12).

He cares for you (1 Pt 5:7).

Parents' prayer

CREATOR, we pause before you in wonder of your workmanship that shaped and formed our precious child, **[insert child's name]**. Thank you for designing him with priceless precision. Not only are his fingerprints an outwardly unique display of his personal identity, but also his heart and soul are imprinted unlike any other. We long to have him become who you intended him to be. For in you, Lord, we live and move and have our being.

Help us to show **[insert child's name]** that he is worthy to be loved and receive love, and that God has called him by name and says, "**[Insert child's name]** you are mine" (Isa 43). Redeem the time we missed in infancy, before he was ours, to build a closer bond and love relationship with **[insert child's name]**.

As we raise **[insert child's name]**, we claim your assurance and peace in all times, including struggles, because you have said do not be anxious about anything, but in everything, pray and give thanks and present your requests to God. We accept your peace for our son and ourselves, which surpasses all understanding (Phil 4:6–7). As we reflect on his story now, help us to tenderly celebrate his life in ways that bring wonder and curiosity, understanding and truth, healing and peace. Bless our work. Help us as we carefully fill the pages of his Lifebook. Prepare **[insert child's name]** to receive his story and protect his heart as he learns his story over the years to come. Amen.

**Now we encourage you to begin writing about
what you have discovered so far:**

If you are truthful, you will be
trusted.

— CONFUCIUS

CHAPTER 7

Truth

Amanda was adopted as an infant, and she always knew she was adopted. Her parents were open and truthful with information when she asked, but she rarely showed any interest. She just wanted to feel the same as, rather than different from, her peers. As an adult today, she is content with who she is and has no plans to find out more information about her birth family until her adoptive parents are gone.

Jayne was adopted as an infant, too. She describes her parents as being open and truthful with what little information they had about her birth family, yet as a child she still experienced fantasies about who they were. While she would have liked more information, she received enough information to satisfy her needs until she began her birth family search at age eighteen.

Tom was adopted as a toddler. His parents rarely discussed his birth history or his Korean heritage. His behavior changed dramatically as a teen and he began abusing drugs and alcohol. He struggled to form an identity as a teen, perhaps for many reasons, including his relinquishment. As a young adult today, he is doing better but continues to struggle. His parents were not educated about the impact of relinquishment and did not recognize the important link between his behavior and his relinquishment. They did not recognize how helpful it could have been for him to know, believe, and understand his birth story.

Longing to know

Why do some adopted children long to know every bit of information they can get a hold of while others are content just knowing what they know? My husband and I are already recognizing how differently each of our three children responds to their relinquishment. Who can predict how they will respond as they process their stories in their own way and over the years to come? Thankfully our children feel comfortable enough to talk with us and ask questions about their adoptions (most of the time). Our comfort level, on the other hand, had to develop over time. Creating a welcoming attitude for their curiosity was the first step, but I am not going to pretend it was easy to take that first step. By introducing adoption language from the beginning, our children knew we were not only happy that we adopted them, but we were willing to talk about it. Yet, the first time I heard the question, "Why did she (birthmother) give me to you?" from our then five-year-old, it startled me. Children have such an honest way with words. As toddlers and preschoolers, our children knew they were adopted, but at that stage in their development, they did not fully understand. However, those younger years helped us to sharpen our skills because, as we discovered, learning how to respond to adoption questions takes practice at any developmental stage.

Over the years we have watched our three children receiving their stories, bit by bit, layer by layer, understanding and not understanding. At their young ages, the information we have been sharing, while important, will not even begin to have full meaning to them until later. But we are laying the groundwork of truth—a firm foundation they will hopefully draw on for years to come.

In this chapter we will discuss reasons and ways to share difficult information with any adopted child. Our prayer is that parents will compassionately reflect on the events surrounding their child's separation and relinquishment from his birth family, often the most difficult piece of an adopted child's story. This part of the journey challenges us to grow through experiencing our feelings about our child's relinquishment in an effort to further prepare us for our role as storyteller. There are varying degrees of difficulty in relinquishment stories, ranging from the understandable and surpassing the unbelievable. Knowing this, we anticipate you may discover emotions you were unaware of. Some may be painful and uncomfortable and some may even deepen your love for your child. Every emotion is okay to feel. It is what you *do* with your feelings that matters. Sit with them. Feel them. Process them.

While it is tempting not to revisit difficult information, do not let that stand in the way of what is important to your child—TRUTH! Parents, we believe that by acknowledging the past we are partnering with God in "uprooting" the effects of relinquishment. All adoptions begin with some degree of loss, and not one of us can predict how, or when, or to what degree that loss may surface. But, we can partner with God, whose wisdom surpasses our understanding, and seek his wisdom because his desire, like ours, is to bring healing and redemption. Author Beth Moore in her book, *Believing God*, writes, "His (God's) motivation for surfacing the destructive parts of us is so we will face them and cooperate as He uproots them and heals our wounds."[1] Suppressing wounds, keeping them from being known, or holding back free expression, is emotionally draining on any child. Megan Bronson, a grief and loss counselor, uses the analogy of a beach ball to describe the energy and unpredictability of holding emotions in. "Holding in feelings and burying our feelings is like holding a beach ball under the water at the lake or a pool—the further you push them down, the more energy it takes to hold them down. Like the beach ball pushed under water, feelings will eventually get away from us and come out on their own—usually in a hurtful or destructive way if one does not take responsibility for their expression."[2] Feelings *will* surface in your child. As parents, we are able to give our children the space and permission to feel and are able to teach them how to manage their emotions. Being an example for our children can be the best form of teaching.

One child we know displayed the impact of his relinquishment wound to his parents early. It surfaced on different occasions (on its own) in feelings of low self-worth, perfectionism, and anger. Otherwise a healthy, loving child, this child was grappling with something inside himself he could not put to words. This family, having worked out the details of his story, was better prepared to offer genuine empathy and understanding when he needed it. They accepted him and his story for what it was and grieved it (felt it), and are helping him to accept it and grieve it as well.

Every child is different though. Some have wounds that stay quietly submerged for years until a life event or some other trigger, such as adolescence or rejection or a significant loss, imposes self-reflection. Some react outwardly through their behavior when they are not able to put words to their feelings. Others move on not knowing how to talk about their birth story because, consciously or innocently, parents block any opportunity for them to explore, ask questions, or imagine safely with them. Many, after knowing their story, seemingly move on contently. So, however your child responds to his story, we encourage you to explore, ask, and imagine with him.

Simplifying difficult information

Some birth parents make loving choices for their children, some clearly feel they have no choice, some are unaware of their choices, others abuse or neglect out of their own brokenness. Whatever the reason for your child's relinquishment situation, having the courage to share it and process it with your child has the greatest potential for making a positive difference in his life. Authors Schooler and Keefer in their book, *Telling the Truth to Your Adopted or Foster Child*, write, "Like everyone else, adoptees need to know where they came from in order to begin to develop a sense of who they are."[3] As storytellers, parents can make the most out of difficult conversations by keeping this and some other simple things in mind.

The list on the next page will be helpful when sharing difficult information with your child.

Children have a limited number of ways of expressing inner distress. Most children under the age of eleven are unlikely to talk freely or at any length about painful feelings. When they are distressed, it is most likely seen in their behavior.[4]

— SHERRIE ELDRIDGE

Be alert to body language

Body language tells us how engaged a child is. It can tell us when a child has had enough. Body language can also show if a child is either comfortable or uncomfortable with what is being said. Body language is a good signal for parents to explore and not ignore. Often you will find submerged emotions. Tune into your child's body language.

When our oldest son entered elementary school, we began talking in more detail about his relinquishment. His initial response was to cover his head with a blanket and hide, signaling to us that he was not only uncomfortable, but wanting to avoid the conversation altogether. Rather than dismiss his feelings, we took the opportunity to help him identify his feelings by asking, "Are you feeling confused?" or "Are you scared?" "Do you know it is okay to feel this way?" This usually brought down the wall—or, in this case, the blanket. We have tried this often and now he seldom covers his head when painful emotions surface. We believe he feels safe to share because we invited and affirmed his feelings. We were honest with him about our own feelings and modeled what we were asking him to do. We helped him put his feelings into words.

If you have a child who displays mixed emotions about his relinquishment through his behavior, stop the conversation and reassure him his feelings are okay. Then, sit with him and listen to his heart.

Timing is everything

Delay difficult conversations brought up by your child in public places such as the grocery store or school. Explain to your child that you will be happy to answer any questions in the car, at home, or in a quieter place where mom or dad can listen better. Do not feel the need to respond on the spot. By explaining you need some time to think about the question before you answer, you send a message of "I care," and will also teach him the importance of timing and safety. This may also provide an opportunity to revisit his Lifebook.

Send an invitation	Do not wait for anniversary dates such as birthdays, "Gotcha Day," or Mother's Day, or Father's Day to talk about story details. While not a daily or weekly event, parents can still be on the lookout for those teachable moments that provide a natural transition into adoption talk. Natural conversations will send the message that you are approachable, normalize your child's experience, and create an environment that welcomes questions at any time.
Quick to listen and slow to speak	Allow your child to *feel* her story, not just *hear* her story—even the not-so-good stuff. Avoid placing any judgment (good or bad) on the people involved in your child's relinquishment story, namely the birth parents. Instead ask her how she feels and what she is thinking. Validate her feelings and help clarify her thoughts. For example, if she feels sad, recognize that feeling by saying, "Yes, that is sad, that makes me sad, too." If she feels angry, allow her to feel it too. Remember, the beach ball may be surfacing. So often, it is the parents who want to avoid the awkwardness when addressing pain, not the children. Again, as the storyteller, it is so important to know your child's story and become aware of and comfortable with your own feelings first. You can only take your child as far as you have gone.
Keep it simple	Share difficult information by using small, simple sentences that are age appropriate for young children. No need to over-explain at a young age. It could create confusion and anxiety. Sharpen your story for a curious school-age child, and "front load," according to author Beth O'Malley, as much information as you can before the teen years. Try to help your child understand difficult details in layers before their childlike trust disappears.
Think ahead	Plan to write the full version of your child's story while details and memories are still fresh. Without a doubt, a completed story ensures our responses will be less awkward when fully rehearsed. Your child will sense your own comfort level and most likely be more receptive. You will also have options regarding what your child is ready to hear and what you are willing to share for her age.

Facing difficult information

We hurt when we know our children have been hurt. This goes for anyone who has ever invested their love in another human being. As an adoptive mother I have had to face my own emotions for my three children's birthmothers and the choices they either made or were forced to make. I have released anger, sadness, and confusion during the making of a Lifebook. When it came to sorting out the difficult information, I felt conflicted inside at first. It was not unusual for me to struggle over each word as I had my heart in one hand and my pen in the other. I am so glad I did it, but it was not easy. In the end I discovered that facing my emotions for what had happened to my children was healthy and freeing. Leaving emotions unresolved has the potential to stir up confusion in the hearts of our children. Sometimes, for the child, this can result in unhealthy methods of communicating or destructive types of behavior.

Whether adoptive parents choose to believe this or not, adoptive children retain an unspoken allegiance to their first set of parents. Often, they have feelings they cannot put to words. Helping them find those words, helping them surface the beach ball without judgment, is a part of the healing that goes on in the uprooting process. Adoption experts find that some children can even develop a "torn allegiance," a type of confusion that sets in between a child's allegiance to her adoptive parents and her birth parents.

If you are holding in secrets, feeling uncomfortable, or are reluctant to share difficult information with your child, we encourage you to face and resolve your emotions regarding the difficult parts of your child's story. Consider the impact on your child when your fears and worries are at the surface ready to burst at the slightest attempt to share difficult information. As they say in the airline industry, "Put the oxygen mask on yourself first before helping your child in the event of a crash." Consider consulting a professional counselor if you need help sharing a painful truth that goes beyond what you can bear. The personal freedom you experience by "going there" will allow courage and hope to grow as you guide your child through her feelings. It is worth it.

Phrasing difficult information

We wanted to share some tips with you for phrasing difficult information in a loving and truthful way. So, we consulted the experts and discovered that the best advice is to keep it simple for younger children and layer the story as your child grows. Dr. Andrew Adesman in his book, *Parenting your Adopted Child*, offers a basic way to discuss the separation. "There are many problematic behaviors and situations including drugs, alcoholism, abuse, poverty, social stigma, and laws that are difficult to talk about but can fall under the general explanation of 'unable to parent.'" In most cases, explaining difficult details in basic language will be the first step and all a child will need and want for a long time. "If she wants more," according to Dr. Adesman, "she will ask."[5]

For a Lifebook, we have included several ways to say and write "unable to parent," although we find ourselves using this phrase often in conversation with our young children. We have collected many general examples including those shared by other adoptive parents. These can be simplified or modified by you with a word change here or there to fit your needs. A general description of the relinquishment story gives a child a chance to respond with questions if she chooses, reinforces that it was not the child's fault, and gives her an opportunity to grow into this difficult part of her story. Finally, these general examples are safe enough to put into a Lifebook without going into specific details. Remember, specific relinquishment details can be brought up in conversation, but are best left out of a Lifebook.

Life was not easy for your birthmother. She had a hard time being a mother. She did not make good choices and that affected her care for you. All babies need love, safety, food, diapers, medicine, and daily care from a responsible adult (or big person). She could not provide these at that time in her life.

Babies love to be held, snuggled, and cared for— they have a special language that tells others they want to feel important and need attention. They need to feel safe and be able to rely on their parents. Your birthmother did not take care of you well after you were born. Since it was important for you to be safe and cared for, other adults made sure you were safe at a time when your birthmother could not.

Your birthmother was not ready to be a mother when you were born. She was only a teenager and unprepared for the responsibilities of parenting a child. She had wonderful support from her family to help her plan a secure future for you through adoption. She had your best interest in mind. She was certain she made the right decision. She felt at peace and gave you to us with a blessing.

Whatever trouble your birthmother had at the time you were born, she wanted better for you. She probably had many questions and concerns. To separate from you was an important decision and, in her mind, she wanted what was right and good for someone as important as you.

Your birthmother was special. She gave you a chance to be with a family forever when she did not believe she could give you a chance on her own. What she did goes beyond that moment she said goodbye. The life you have today is because she chose life for you. You mattered.

She did not treat you well because she was not well. When she was not thinking clearly because of alcohol, drugs, or despair, she was not safe for you. You were taken to a foster home where you could have what babies needed to be healthy.

Your Chinese birthmother *(knew)* or *(was told)* she could not keep you *[parents can explain all the reasons in China that may apply]* and placed you where you would be found quickly by grownups. In her heart, it was important for you to have a good life. We believe she was relieved to know you were safe and cared for. Birthmothers do not want to be forgotten. We believe she will never forget you, and we will never forget her.

Your birthmother could not provide for herself and a baby. She did not have a husband or family to help her. This is very hard and it is the reason she wanted something more for you. She wanted you to have a healthy life. You are a very important person to her and to us.

Your birthmother was not married. Unmarried mothers face big problems in some countries if they choose to keep their babies *[insert child's birth country and explain social issues]*. In her mind it was the best but hardest choice to place you for adoption.

Your birthmother was sorry she could not raise you. She did the best she could. She carried you in her tummy (womb) safely until you were born. With great responsibility she considered what was best for you rather than what was best for her. It hurt to say goodbye to someone so precious. Yet, she wanted you to be where you are today—with us.

In summary

It is so important to find a way to deliver any difficult information in a way that does not excuse the need for the separation. Do not try to hide the pain of relinquishment. As authors Schooler and Keefer write, "The only way out is through."[6] Make assumptions where information is sketchy as long as they are reasonable.

When you write, clearly put the responsibility where it belongs. Write that it was not your child's fault. Dr. Andrew Adesman warns that the fear of wondering, "Is it my fault?" is so common that parents should bring this up at least once, even if your child never mentions it to you.[7] Remember to write an age-appropriate response using simple sentences if your child is small and use greater detail if your child is older. Create appropriate boundaries when deciding what difficult information to include in print. Whatever you write, keep information factual and free of personal judgment, but feel free to verbally share your emotions in a healthy way. May God meet you and comfort you as you allow yourself to authentically embrace your feelings about your child's story.

HOMEWORK

details

Questionnaire 2 — Truth

Review court and/or legal documents prior to beginning this section.

Relinquishment details

1. Write down any information or assumptions about the birth parents' situation. Consider economic, political, and cultural issues when applicable. Consider social issues, emotional issues, poor choices, and other reasons they were not able to parent. For example, "Children need to be safe," or "Adults were not safe," or "They were teen parents."

2. What is the role of a responsible parent, and did birth parents fulfill their responsibility?

3. Do you know or can you assume any thoughts of the birth parents during the pregnancy? Were they planning for your child's future—anxious, agonizing over choices they had to make, hoping for a better life for their child, overwhelmed by the enormity of the situation?

4. Were there any other adults involved in this decision (courts, Child Protective Services, legal guardian, adoption or social worker, supportive parents, foster parents)?

5. Why did the birth parents relinquish their child for adoption?

6. Explain to your child that she was not at fault.

7. Explain to your child what you believe God's heart was for her in the midst of this separation.

8. What promises spoken in the Bible can you claim for your child? Refer to list of Scriptures on the following page.

Claim it

"You can clutch the past so tightly to your chest that it leaves your arms too full to embrace the present."

— JAN GLIDEWELL

scripture

See, I am sending an angel ahead of you to guard you along the way and to bring you to the place I have prepared (Ex 23:20).

Behold, I make all things new (Rv 21:5 NKJV).

He has made everything beautiful in its time (Eccl 3:11).

Truly my soul finds rest in God; my salvation comes from him. Truly he is my rock and my salvation; he is my fortress, I will never be shaken (Ps 62:1–2).

The Lord bless you and keep you; the Lord make his face shine on you and be gracious to you; the Lord turn his face toward you and give you peace (Nm 6:24–26).

Put on the full armor of God (Eph 6:1).

And we know that in all things God works for those who love
him, who have been called according to his purpose (Rom 8:28).

Personal prayer

LORD, our child, **[child's name]**, like us, was born in this
less than perfect world. **[Child's name]** began her life
in a way you would not have chosen for her. The cause
was not from you but from the brokenness in this world. But
you made it right with her and brought her to the very place
she is today. As questions are asked of us about that journey,
we ask for wisdom and direction to respond in a truthful, age-
appropriate way. May you speak tenderness and compassion
through us. May you access the young, wounded places of
[child's name]'s heart, and when she wrestles with the impact
of relinquishment, we ask that you meet her in those deep
places and heal any brokenness that comes from the wound of
being relinquished. We long for **[child's name]** to grieve well.
Help us uproot any doubt, irrational thoughts, fear, confusion,
or anxiety she may hold and may we help her reprocess it in a
healthy way. May her relinquishment and adoption not define
her nor make her feel devalued or insignificant in any way. We
pray that you will continue to work in **[child's name]** in such a
way that she would fulfill her purpose here on earth. We pray
that **[child's name]** will have a strong sense of security in our
family and know to the deepest part of her being that she
is truly loved. Thank you, Jesus, that you have come to set
[child's name] free from her past. We pray that she will always
understand that you were involved in her story, and may she
continue to see traces of your movement in her life. Amen.

Practicing writing here:

To look backward for a while is to refresh the eye, to restore it, and to render it the more fit for its prime function of looking forward.[1]

— MARGARET FAIRLESS BARBER

Honor birth parents in your child's presence.[2]

— SHERRIE ELDRIDGE

CHAPTER 8

Honor

When I first read the children's adoption book, *Did My First Mother Love Me?*[3] I had no idea my emotions about my son's birthmother were so close to the surface. As I read each page my eyes welled up with tears. As I was reading this book to our three-year-old (our first child) he was sitting quietly on my lap wondering why Mommy was crying. As much as I was taken by surprise by my emotional response, our son, too, was processing his own emotions. Not about his birthmother, at least I did not think so. He was too young for that. He was worrying about me. Doing my best to conceal my tears did not help, either. Our son had decided, if this book made Mommy cry, then we should never read it again. I learned an important lesson that day. Explore your emotions about your child's birthmother/birth parents in a healthy way, and preferably before visiting the story with him. Then, when talking with your child about his birth parents, you will be able to better empathize with him. It is important to be able to authentically affirm your child's emotions. At a young age, children can become easily and unnecessarily confused by feelings they cannot process accurately at this stage in their development. They will need your help. For me, a children's book was the trigger that began releasing my emotions. Will there be a trigger for you?

So began my connection with our birthmothers. Not physically, but emotionally and spiritually. At first, I did not know how to process my feelings about each of them. I felt differently about them all. In the beginning it was hard to imagine who they were—their characters, the pressures in their lives, the stress, and the enormity of it all. What had they considered before releasing each child for adoption? Do they love the child they are now separated from? Is it possible they think of them? Is it possible they think only about themselves? With just a few basic facts about each of them scattered on poorly translated court documents, my feelings were hard to discern at first. I struggled. There was a big disconnect I had to deal with. We had never had birthmothers before, and now we had three.

Trying to get connected

Reading the word ABANDONED in really big letters stamped on court documents certainly did not help me connect. In fact, I lived with the thought of abandonment for so long that I was not sure I liked what this birthmother did. Knowing she abandoned her child certainly did not endear her to me. "How could a mother do this to her child?" I thought. After reading the children's book, *Did My First Mother Love Me?* I had a whole new perspective to consider. I began to feel her pain. My tears were grieving her loss and my child's loss. I hated the abandonment, but I began to see this woman and her actions differently. I began to see her story through *her* eyes. I believe God was nudging me to take a closer look at her heart. Is it possible that she could not bear to put her child through the challenges she faced by keeping him at that time in her life? Is it possible any other choice would have been irresponsible or shameful? What about the relief she may have felt when she saw he was safely born? These thoughts began to replace my initial impression of her. I wanted to know more.

By the time we adopted our second and third child, I knew better than to jump to negative conclusions so quickly. But what does one think when an unmarried birthmother does not show up in court to claim not one but three little girls? I questioned her capacity to parent, and then I realized maybe she did, too. What could she be trapped in? Is it possible she knew somewhere deep in her heart that it would be better for her children to be taken since her own life was out of control at that time? Could she no longer keep them safe? It may not have been selfless or mature, but not showing up was apparently what was best at the time. I believe many hearts were broken that day the girls were taken away. The girls will be told the truth and it will be hard, but in doing so, they will also know it was not their fault. The truth that people are not perfect will be tough for them to grasp and accept. Forgiveness may take time.

It's hard to imagine what it would be like not to be able to feed my child. It's hard to imagine what it would be like to be trapped in an out-of-control lifestyle. It's hard to imagine living in a culture that shuns or rejects both the single mother and the child potentially for the rest of their lives. It's hard to imagine not seeing my child ever again.

I spoke with other adoptive moms about their feelings for their children's birth parents. Not surprisingly, most had comments only about birthmothers. So we will take a look at that first and talk about birthfathers later in the chapter.

One adoptive mom shared this story about her two domestically adopted children with much emotion. "I believe they (birthmothers) did the right thing. They loved them enough to know they could not care for them. They could have chosen other solutions, but they chose life. They both planned for their children's futures even though they were not going to be physically a part of it. They each picked a family. They each signed important papers that secured a family. They each had good prenatal care. One even stopped taking drugs while pregnant. They did a good job making sure each child was going to be okay, especially when no one was really in their lives to support or help them through such a decision." It became important for this adoptive mother to look for the good in the character of her children's birthmothers. She developed new eyes to see that these women deserved her honor and respect.

A mother of an adopted child from China wrote this in her daughter's Lifebook, and I paraphrase, "Your birth parents kept you and loved you and cared for you as long as they could. When they could no longer take care of you, they decided to take you to a place where they knew you would be taken care of. They dressed you in warm clothes and placed you in a bamboo basket and set you at the front gate of the child welfare institution knowing that someone would find you and take you inside."

This adoptive mom and others are quick to defend their children's birthmothers' choices to "place" their children rather than to call it abandonment. Many conclude, "This is the only adoption plan available, at high risk, to Chinese birthmothers. This is their relinquishment plan." Once again, this adoptive mother highlighted the important role and action of the birthmother.

In her book *The Lost Daughters of China*,[4] Karin Evans imagines her newly adopted daughter's Chinese mother, her emotions upon placing her child in a busy marketplace, the sights, smells, sounds of the market, and the amplified cries of a baby separated from the only source of comfort and love she knew. For this birthmother — as for many others in China—hopes and dreams vanish at the separation from her child. Laws, poverty, traditions, and the threat of punishment—not the heart—dictate decisions in most cases. Other countries with similar social or economic pressures cause many birthmothers to make heartbreaking choices. We must remember, choosing to place a child for adoption is not easy. There is so much more to the story.

We believe birthmother stories need to be closely examined, especially in closed adoptions where information is too scarce to draw the best conclusions. If the birthmother story is not more fully developed, then adoptive parents run the risk of talking about this important story with their child in an unhealthy way. We encourage parents to tell your child's birthmother story in an honoring way—for her sake and for your child's sake.

Reality check

Some birth parent stories are tragic and some children have been traumatized, abused, or neglected by birth parents. The lack of love is truly heartbreaking. Sherrie Eldridge adds, "I think the large majority of birthmothers love their babies, but the reality is that some don't."[5] If you have a story that you are struggling with and a child who has been traumatized, abused, or neglected prior to adoption, again we recommend seeking a trained professional to help you and your child sort out her story in a truthful, age-appropriate, and healthy way. Hiding a traumatic story may seem safe, but walking through it, together with your child, has the potential to create greater understanding and emotional freedom for both you and your child.

Ignorance is not bliss

What do we do with this knowledge about birth parents? Well, someday our children may wonder what their birth parents were like, whether they did something wrong or right, and whether or not they think about the children they relinquished. Many adopted children have questions, and your truthful assessment and sharing about the birth parents may be your son's or daughter's only chance of ever knowing about them. Therefore, adoptive parents should try their best to empathically connect with the birth parent story and learn how to honor this second set of parents and their contribution to who our sons and daughters are today. We know we have already emphasized this, but it bears repeating. Connecting with them does not mean approving of any irresponsible behavior, should that be the case. Rather, it deepens and brings understanding to the child's story for both the adoptive parents and the adopted child. A truthful story is critical for our sons or daughters to fully understand why he or she is not with this first set of parents, and understanding is an important part of the process of healing.

Because birth parents have played and may (in open adoptions) continue to play some sort of role in the lives of our children, we can help our children to know a number of things so that they can imagine them in a healthy way. For example, birth parent genes contribute talents, physical looks such as skin color, eye shape and color, and hair texture, to name a few. Occasionally we have taken the time to wonder with our children and point out a trait one might share with a birth parent. For instance, our oldest son loves music. We imagine with him that one of his birth parents may have loved music because we see such a love for music in him. Our daughter has a flare for drama. We have been fortunate to find and meet her two older birth sisters and we see it in them too. We can safely assume this comes from her birth family because it does not come from us. When we do this, we are not dredging up the past unnecessarily, but rather, we are working with it. If we adoptive parents believe we can claim all a child is and will become, we are not only being dishonest with everyone involved, but we are not helping our children develop a healthy sense of self and connection to their birth parents. If a child knows she is adopted, then she knows she has two sets of parents. It is then our job to occasionally point out to them similarities to and differences from both sets of parents.

Another way we can help our children better understand their birth parents is to compassionately discuss with them troubling information about their birth parents. Connecting emotionally with the birth parent story, as I related that I did with ours in the first part of this chapter, can add a new perspective to a story or simply reaffirm what one already knows. An occasional conversation with your child about troubling information is likely to be hard at first. However, these conversations do benefit a child and remind him that, "It was not his fault."

Missing information

Can it help to discuss missing information? Yes! In many cases there is a lot of missing information about birth parents that may never be known. Yet talking about missing information is important for the child. Even acknowledging that which we do not know opens the door for healing conversation. We may not know their names or what they look like, but it is important to say, sensitively, "We do not know." Beware, however, that an older child may not be satisfied with that reply and will continue to press for more details. One adult adoptee said, "I don't have any personal stories about my birthmother. All I remember my adoptive parents telling me is that there could be many reasons why she chose to put me up for adoption [this was in the 1970s] … maybe she died, or was too sick to care for me, or decided that she was not able to care for me appropriately, or she was just too young." The fact is that the unknown leaves questions in a child's mind. It has the potential to deaden imagination, create unnecessary vivid imagination, or sometimes even send a message to the child that certain parts of her story are not important. Sometimes, though, the specific reasons for relinquishment are truly unknown. The information is indeed missing. This can create tension, and we all know that feeling tension isn't always comfortable for us. Sitting *in* the tension, though, has the ability to take us somewhere good and valuable. Being honest about the lack of specific information matters. Acknowledging and holding the tension can change us. We encourage you to sit *in* that tension *with* your child.

Making safe assumptions

Making safe assumptions is another healthy way to connect our children with their birth parents, but it has to be done well. Some of the information you provide to your child will be based on facts and others based on assumptions. When you make safe assumptions about birth parents, state clearly that they *are* assumptions. Using words such as, "we assume, we can only guess, or we wonder," are some of the ways to articulate vague or unknown details. In contrast, "We do not know her name" or "We do not know if they were married" are examples of facts. Again, be clear with your child about the difference and be sure to add both positive and difficult details to the story when relevant.

A word about birthfathers

It may sound odd to mention this, but every child has a birthfather, adopted children too. Yet birthfathers are often overlooked in the making of a Lifebook for a couple of reasons. Often there is a lot of missing information about them, and it becomes tricky to explain how a man and a woman, possibly unmarried, had sex that perhaps resulted in an unplanned pregnancy. In spite of all this, it will still be important to acknowledge the father and the events that took place that resulted in his being your child's birthfather. Here is why: Omitting details such as this may lead to uncertainty or hurtful assumptions by the child. According to Jana Wolff in *Secret Thoughts of an Adoptive Mother*, "The only thing worse than bad news is no news."[6] In the end, concrete facts about birthfathers or any part of the birth parent story sprinkled with safe assumptions may provide all the information that a child will ever want or need. Here is a brief excerpt from a Lifebook, belonging to a young girl adopted from Korea, about her birthfather.

Your birthfather was twenty-five and your birthmother was twenty-three when you were born. We do not know their names. They both had jobs and we believe they worked long hours and earned little money. We are not sure what types of jobs they had. They lived in the city and each had their own place to live. They dated. Young couples enjoy being together when they date. While they were dating, you were conceived. That means they made a baby and that baby was you. Your birthfather was probably afraid when your birthmother told him she was pregnant. It was then and is now unacceptable in their country for unmarried couples to have and keep babies. They most likely talked about you and what they would do. Even though he knew about you, he probably worried about a lot of things, especially how he could be a father. He may not have had anyone in his life he could count on for help or guidance. His family may have made him feel ashamed. We think he did not know what do to. At that time in his life he could not work things out and he ran from the situation. Your birthmother had a safe pregnancy and we thank God for her and for giving you life. After you were born she placed you in the caring arms of responsible adults she could count on because she knew she could not parent you alone. If your birthfather knew you now, we know he would be very proud of you.

Many birth parents face pressures either imposed by their culture or self-imposed by the reality of their life situations. Rarely is the decision by both birth parents to give up a child lacking emotion. "Allowing another family to adopt her child is undoubtedly one of the hardest decisions a human being can make."[7] Sometimes the *best* thing is the hardest thing and yet the most loving thing. Are you starting to connect differently with your child's birth parents?

During times of wondering—a spiritual connection

"Does my birthmother think about me? Does she miss me? Does she know I am adopted, safe, and happy?" These are some of the common questions adopted children have and wonder about their birth parents. We have heard our children ask these very questions. "Yes," we say. "This was what she wanted for you." Or "Yes, she misses you. It is hard for anyone to 'unthink' about someone so important." We suggest to adoptive parents in times of wondering to encourage their child to talk to God about their feelings and to pray for their birth parents. One adoptive mom wrote this prayer in her daughter's Lifebook and it went something like this:

> *And if you find yourself thinking about your birthmother, you can pray this simple prayer. "Lord, Jesus, I am thinking about my birthmother. I want her to know I am fine. Please comfort her if I am in her thoughts, too. Amen."*

Another mother wrote that when her daughter has questions about her birthmother, they talk and also pray together. "For example," she wrote, "when wondering or worrying if her birthmother knows that she is okay, we say a prayer together and ask God to fill her birthmother's heart with reassurance. We can then talk about how nothing is too hard for God and that she will get the message somehow."

Not only can we pray with our children as a way of connecting them to their birth parents, but it is also a loving way to help them learn to share their questions, worries, and concerns to us and the Lord. Teaching our children to pray in the moment models the type of relationship God desires to have with us. This may require some to think of God in a new way—that he is relational and meets us and our children where we are at. We can be real with God.

In summary

A birthmother will always somehow be mysteriously connected with her relinquished child. Bonding naturally occurs in the womb. However, in his book, *Adoptees Come of Age*, Ron Nydam points out that, "Few adoptees rarely see how love and abandonment could fit together."[8] Left on their own to imagine who their birth parents were and what they did is to leave a child with a story that is unshaped from many sides. Adoptive parents can paint a fuller birth parent picture of the first chapter in a child's life. By doing this, they may help their child avoid serious struggles with identity, while at the same time affirming his identity in his Creator. The miracle of adoption is an expression of how God participates in the restoration and healing of our lives and our stories. It is no mistake that your child is in your home. He is right where he is supposed to be.

As a birth parent counselor once told us, "I don't think most birthmothers want to be forgotten. They want to have their children accept the adoption as a positive choice ... The more open the adoptive parents are with their children about birth families and the relinquishment, usually the better."[9]

May you be challenged with a new way of thinking about your child's birth parents and find a new way of connecting with and honoring them.

HOMEWORK

honor

Questionnaire 3 — Honor

"One problem we do see in many Lifebooks," according to an email we received from Dr. Greg Keck, "is that the WHOLE truth is omitted; often the HOLE truth (some of the truth with many holes) is what exists."[10] Be honest so that your child is not left wondering why he is not with these people today. Do not confuse your child by boiling down his relinquishment and his birth parents actions in the name of love. This can undermine a child's view of love and prevent him from ever loving fully in fear that it will go away just as it did when he was born. Finally, decide how you will refer to the birth parents. For example, birthmother, birthfather, Chinese mother, lady whose tummy you grew in, or by their first names. Reserve endearing terms like "mommy" and "daddy" only for you.

Allow yourself some time to pray before working on this questionnaire.

1. Birthmother's full name.

2. Birthfather's full name.

3. Marital status at time of relinquishment.

4. Birthmother's date of birth and age at child's birth.

5. Birthfather's date of birth and age at child's birth.

6. Physical description of birthmother.

7. Physical description of birthfather.

8. What character traits can you safely assume of birthmother?

9. What character traits can you safely assume of birthfather?

10. Birth parent life circumstances.

11. Any family/friend support to birth parents?

12. Occupations at time of relinquishment.

13. How was the adoption plan carried out (placed, contacted attorney, found on busy street corner, agency, social services)?

14. Do you believe your child's birthmother valued life? How do you know this?

15. Did the birthmother see or hold her baby?

16. Typical housing birth family may have lived in (description or photo).

17. Map of town, city, province, region birth parents were from.

18. Where are they today?

19. Any memories from child of birth parents?

20. Any memories from child of birth home?

21. Any memories from child of birth relatives?

22. What talents, interests, looks, eye color, skin color, etc., did your child receive from birth parents?

23. What clues did your child's birth parents leave to show that their intentions were good and that they loved and cared for their child? Wrapped in warm clothes when abandoned (placed), evidence of good prenatal care, journal, letters, money?

24. What clues or evidence did your child's birth parents show upon placement, abandonment or other that their intentions were not healthy at that time for the child?

25. Do you have a faith story that you would like to share with your child that shows God's intentions to bring your family together through adoption? What are you especially thankful for?

26. Explain how well you will help your child understand why he/she is not with his/her first set of parents so that he/she understands the choices were made for his/her well-being and future. What do you and your child want to say to his/her birthmother?

Claim it

scripture

Be kind and compassionate to one another, forgiving each other, just as in Christ God forgave you (Eph 4:32).

You wisely and tenderly lead me, and then you bless me (Ps 73:24 MSG).

The secret things belong to the LORD our God ... (Dt 29:29).

The peace of God, which transcends all understanding, will guard your hearts and your minds in Christ Jesus (Phil 4:7).

For God has not given us a spirit of fear, but of power and of love and of a sound mind (2 Tm 1:7).

Who shall separate us from the love of Christ? (Rom 8:35).

I can do all things through Christ who strengthens me (Phil 4:13 NKJV).

The Lord will fulfill his purpose for me ... (Ps 138:8 ESV).

Call to me and I will answer you. I'll tell you marvelous and won-drous things that you could never figure out on your own (Jer 33:3 MSG).

Wait for the LORD; be strong and take heart and wait for the LORD (Ps 27:14).

And we know that in all things God works for the good of those who love him, who have been called according to his purpose (Rom 8:28).

You have put gladness in my heart (Ps 4:7 NKJV).

Sing a new song to the Lord. For he has done great things (Ps 98:1a NLV).

Personal prayer

FATHER, it is our desire to learn how to honor **[insert child's name]**'s birth parents in his presence and in the pages of his Lifebook. Yet we find it difficult and confusing to digest the painful pieces of information given to us about them. Help us to suspend any preconceived notions and judgments we have already made about them based on little or no information. Give us the wisdom needed to develop a fuller understanding of who his birth parents are—their emotions, their character, and their heart. You have indirectly put these birth parents into our lives. One day, **[insert child's name]** may want to know more about them, maybe even search for them. Show us an honest picture of who these first parents are, the good and the bad, and may we not forget that we, ourselves, are a picture of brokenness and redemption. Thank you for specifically choosing us to continue the parenting that **[insert child's name]** not only needs, but deserves. We pray that our son will be able to forgive all the adults in his life who could not stay with him. We pray for his emotional needs as we try to imagine how vulnerable he may be to thoughts and feelings of rejection and abandonment by adults who could not remain in his life. During times of wondering or worry may he seek and receive your comfort and counsel. We pray that **[insert child's name]**'s birthmother and/or birthfather has reconciled her/his decision to relinquish him and is reassured that her/his child is in a safe place. May you assure both parents with the peace of knowing that their child is deeply loved. Amen.

Practice writing here:

Tell me and I forget; show me and
I remember; involve me and I
understand.

—UNKNOWN

CHAPTER 9

Explore

Our children developed a desire to know about their birth histories through the real places, real people, and real events they heard about and were shown in their Lifebooks. You have probably guessed by now that we have cultivated their interest on purpose, not by accident. We had a choice to forget about it or discover it. We chose to discover as much as we could and felt by doing so we could really help them know and believe their stories. We also discovered that exploring together allowed us to grow closer together. Our children were not left wondering where we stood regarding this part of their life.

> Scripture reminds us to come
> alongside one another and to
> "encourage one another and
> build each other up."
>
> — 1 THESSALONIANS 5:11

On the contrary, a lot of what you will discover in this chapter has often been overlooked by adoptive parents, who perhaps believe the past is better left in the past or is unimportant. After all, they might think, most adopted children appear to lack interest in these things. But, do they? While it is true some children are curious and some are not, as parents we are able to teach our children to be curious and give them permission want to know more. The little things can often make the biggest difference. The little things can make a big, confusing concept clearer. So, let's continue preparing to cultivate a healthy curiosity in our children as they grow.

In the next six questionnaires, we provide a guide for you to follow as think through what else needs to be included in your child's Lifebook. Of course it is impossible for us to ask all the questions that could possibly cover every situation, so we encourage you to include questions of your own. After each questionnaire, sit with the information for a while. Imagine what you will write. Practice writing a few lines at a level your child will understand. Or, we suggest you write for a child who is elementary school age, approximately seven to nine years old, remembering children at this age can grasp more and generally have more interest. These questionnaires are also provided in a logical format to help you sequentially tell the story. Based on our experience, this format is proven, but open to improvement should you want to add your own creative expression.

HOMEWORK

explore

What details can you share that appear on your child's original birth certificate or other important documents? Most important for this section is to display a copy of your child's birth certificate if you have one. If you do not, consider what documents you can display in this section that will help confirm your child's story such as abandonment papers, medical records, or finding ads. Remember, it is up to you what documents you choose to include or not to include.

Questionnaire 4 — Important documents

1. Do you have a copy of your child's original birth certificate to put in his Lifebook? If not, write that you do not have an original birth certificate and the reasons why you do not.

2. If you do not have an original birth certificate, consider what you can display in this section that will help confirm your child's birth, such as medical records, abandonment papers, etc.

3. Do you have an English translation of your child's birth certificate or other important documents? Make copies to display side-by-side on the Lifebook page.

4. Explain any information found on the birth certificate or other important documents. For example, underneath or near the document, write, "This is your original birth certificate. Your birthmother and birthfather's names are on this certificate. It tells the place and date you were born."

5. Is the information true or fabricated? For example, "This information is not true because ..." or "We know the information is accurate because ..." and fill in the reasons why.

Why is it important?

These documents will give concrete and visual proof that your child was born. The information in these documents can confirm what is real and what is not. (Note: Experts suggest that parents only include contact information for birth parents if you currently have an open relationship with safe boundaries.)

Practice writing here:

HOMEWORK

facts and info

Questionnaire 5 — Reporting laws and more

If you have information about the laws, social pressures, and/or societal norm specific to your child's birth country that will help clarify decisions made by birth parents, you may wish to answer the following questions.

1. Describe the process the birth parents went through that made your child available for adoption.

2. What significant cultural attitudes, ancient traditions, social stigmas, government laws, or fines may have played a role in the birth parents' choices/decisions?

Transition process

1. Who helped the birth parents with their adoption plan during this overwhelming time? For example, an adoption agency, close friends, specific relatives, social services? Perhaps there was no one to help. What important documents were signed? In the absence of facts, what can you safely assume?

2. Where do babies live and who cares for them after they are born and before they are adopted? For example, foster family, baby home, or orphanage.

3. What assurances were given to the birth parents to know their child would be safe and cared for? In the absence of facts, what can you safely assume?

Why is it important?

Reporting laws, social stigmas, cultural pressures, and societal norms that played a part in your child's story can help put things into perspective for her. This layer of the story should be included in a Lifebook, but told in general terms until a child is old enough to understand. For example, for a young child you might say, "After you were born, you were placed in the arms of caring, responsible adults who knew exactly what to do." You could include a picture of the adoption worker, foster mother, or caregiver holding your child. For a child who is capable of understanding difficult concepts, such as why her birth country does things differently or has different beliefs and values or why things are acceptable or merely tolerated, you can go into greater detail. This will give meaning and understanding to the many reasons children are placed for adoption. Becoming the storyteller means you are prepared in advance with the knowledge your child will need both now and in the future.

Finally, when you report this piece of your child's story, make sure you report what was going on at the time your child was placed for adoption. Perhaps circumstances have changed. For example, our children are not old enough to understand that when they were adopted the Russian health care system was crumbling, and the standard of living was falling. The Russian economy was and still remains in crisis.[1] One way we can help now is to collect magazine, newspaper, and Internet articles that truthfully reflect the situation their birth parents may have faced that contributed to their decisions.

Practice writing here:

Birth sibling curiosity

A child may be curious about birth siblings and whether or not she has any, and some may not. If your child has a birth sibling, there are some things you can do to honor this relationship in a Lifebook. When we adopted our youngest, we discovered she was separated from her two older birth sisters. It did not take long for us to decide to find them. But, to our surprise, when we made our inquiry, they were not to be found. Before long we learned they had been adopted, too. We were pleased but still longed to locate them for our daughter's sake. Once we learned that they were in the United States it took only three days on the Internet to locate them. Now, we have met and enjoy exchanging letters, photos, presents, and updates. We collect and insert many of these treasures in our daughter's Lifebook.

Our sons' birth siblings were living with their birth parents or relatives at the time of their adoptions. We have no contact with them. Talking about these siblings can be a sensitive thing for us. What do we say when one of them asks, "Do they know about me?" or "Do they miss me?" It is important, however uncomfortable the parent is, to talk about birth siblings because it is honest.

Joey Nesler in her article, "Questions about Birth Siblings," suggests that adoptive parents get comfortable with this information before discussing it in an age-appropriate way. "When responding to your child, use non-reactive, honest, age appropriate language." She continues, "A hushed tone conveys secrecy or shame, while an elevated tone can suggest anxiety."[2] Making a sibling page in a Lifebook should offer you the chance to get comfortable with what you either know or can assume. According to adoption experts, the appropriate time to tell about siblings is when a child is approximately seven or eight years old. For parents with younger children, that gives plenty of time to prepare. For others with school-age children, you will find help in the following questionnaire. As always, we suggest you complete this information as it fits your child's situation. For example, should you make a toddler book, capture sibling information and file it for a later date. If you are ready to include it, go for it.

HOMEWORK

birth siblings

Questionnaire 6—Birth Siblings

1. To your knowledge, does your child have birth siblings? If yes, what are their names and ages, and with whom and where do they live? If no, or if you
    are uncertain, write this as your answer.

2. What is the age difference between the sibling(s) and your child?

3. Why do you think these siblings are with the birth family and your child is not? For example, birthmothers make decisions for different reasons, depending on the circumstances they are in. Explain for example, "She was able to parent your brother because things were different for her then." Explain what was different. For example, she was older, she had help from other people, laws were different.

4. If you are not in contact with the birth sibling(s), what can you assume about them based on what "most" children do at this age in that particular county, state, city? For example, do they go to school, work, have friends, play, help in the home, watch TV?

5. What does your child have in common with the sibling(s)? A family resemblance, similar interests, talents, personality, physical features.

6. What could be different about your child and his/her siblings? For example, language, what they eat, what they learn in school, personality, physical features.

Why is it important?

Some children may never have a desire to do anything with the information they learn about a sibling. That is okay. It is a piece of their history and who they are and the awareness may be all they need or want. Knowing about a sibling does not mean they must establish a relationship with them. Where contact is available and desired by the child, as parents, you make the same wise, safe decisions you would make for anyone your child wishes to hang out with.

Practice writing here:

Birth place information

Research has never been easier than it is today. With search engines that can connect you with just about any information, there is so much you can discover about your child's place of birth. Of course your local library remains a wonderful source for children's books and videos with topics ranging from recipes, poetry, religion, history, culture, and daily living. Surprise your child with how much you know about where he/she was born. Inspire him/her to explore too. What is different, unique, or similar to your home? This is a good time to partner with other adoptive parents to share resources.

HOMEWORK

your child's place of birth

Questionnaire 7—Place of Birth

1. What is the name of the city/town and state/ province where your child was born? Describe it. Compare it to where you live now. How is it the same or how is it different? Is it large, small, rural, urban?

2. Describe the country's historical highlights, economy, traditions, arts, religion, food, sports, housing, people, hobbies, schools, music, TV shows, jobs, recreation.

3. Select and display important visuals such as maps, flag, time zone, weather information.

4. What do most children do in the nation, state, or city for fun?

5. What memories does your child have of his/her birth place?

6. What memories do you have of your child's birth place?

7. What typical family traditions can you discover? What holidays do they celebrate? What traditional costumes/clothing do they wear?

8. What values and beliefs do you share in common? What is different?

Why is it important?

It is important for parents to help their child imagine his place of birth because it is another piece of his story and identity. Learning that it is okay to embrace one's roots gives permission to a child to embrace and feel proud of his past. It normalizes it, too. Not to introduce his birth place may say to a child that this part of him is not important.

Practice writing here:

HOMEWORK

family and feelings

Questionnaire 8—Becoming a family

1. What words have been placed on your heart that best describes how and when your child joined your family through adoption?

2. How did you prepare to become parents?

3. How did God prepare your hearts?

4. How did you pray for your child while you awaited his/her arrival? For example, did you pray for God to prepare his/her heart to bond with yours, or to provide peace for him/her during separation, or to surround him/her with caring and nurturing caregivers?

5. What about protecting him/her while in the womb?

6. What were the highlights of your adoption story? What were the low points?

7. What can you tell your child about how you faced many challenges to become a family and how together you will work through any difficulty?

8. How will you display your joy and unconditional love for him/her? Reinforce for your child that he/she belongs with your family.

Why is it important?

This is a great place to share some of the processes and feelings you went through as waiting adoptive parents and/or family and to tell of the adoption journey itself. Your child may ask questions about what made you decide to adopt and what it was like as you prepared for her arrival. If you kept a journal, review it for answered prayers and blessings. It is important for her to know and understand that choosing her to become a part of your family was intentional. Knowing she was not a mistake and that she fulfilled a desire in your heart and in God's plan will be treasured by her forever. Everyone longs to belong. Maybe you gave birth before and/or after you decided to adopt. Your child may wonder if you love her as if she was your biological child. It is important that your child knows and hears your heart and how you arrived at your decisions.

Practice writing here:

Now I know who I am!

Now that we have looked at your child's story, think about who he is today. For sure he has developed his own personality, style, likes, and dislikes. You will want to continue to capture "who he is" at various stages in his life. Watch and listen to how his answers and interests will change depending on his age. Repeat this quiz with him as a preschooler, school age, preteen (tween), and teenager. These pages of a Lifebook are meant to be completed *with* your child. Have fun celebrating who he is!

HOMEWORK

this is who I am

Questionnaire 9—Who I am

1. How old are you?

2. What is your favorite color?

3. What is your favorite game?

4. What is your favorite food?

5. What is your favorite song?

6. What is your favorite thing to do?

7. Who are your best friends?

8. What school do you attend?

9. What is your favorite school subject?

10. What do you want to be when you grow up?

11. Are you a daughter or son, sister, or brother?

12. Describe your family.

Parents may need to answer these questions with their own healthy observations until a child is old enough.

HOMEWORK

this is who I am

Who is in your family?

What are the names of siblings, relatives, pets?

How are you the same as your family?

How are you different from your family?

How are you the same as your birth family?

How are you different from your birth family?

What is your ethnicity, nationality, culture?

What are your family's favorite traditions?

What three words best describe you?

What are your favorite childhood memories?

What talents do you have?

What are you thankful for?

Why do you think you were adopted?

What age-appropriate things can you and your child collect for her Lifebook now and as she grows older? Here are a few ideas:

Current photos

Artwork

Handwritten name

Stickers

Handprint

Friends who are adopted

Does your child have any friends who are adopted? Up-to-date information about your child's friend(s) with adoptive backgrounds can be included in his Lifebook. Sharing this common bond is valuable and helps normalize the adoption experience. Include current photos of each friend as well as pre-adoption baby or toddler photos.

Note: Teenagers have their own opinion of what is and is not cool for their book. Find out what makes your teen tick and what types of things would be meaningful for him to include in his Lifebook.

Finally, what comments can you (and other family members) add that best describe everyone's feelings about your child today?

Why is it important?

Part of what makes up your child's identity are the very things that make them distinct as a daughter or son, as a brother or sister, as a student, as a friend, their likes and dislikes, their mannerisms, their physical features, their style, their skills and abilities, etc. It is important to highlight these special features in a Lifebook as they continue to develop into the person God has created them to be. Creating an environment that affirms who your child is and how he bears the image of God is essential and needs to be celebrated.

Conclusion

Our concluding thoughts on this chapter are short and sweet. Sit with the information you have gathered. Sit with all of it for a few days. Look at it, circle it, underline it, modify it, and then look at it again. Pray about it. Get physical and place it on the floor and ask God to look at it. Remember how God wants to partner with you throughout this process. May he bless this important work.

Claim it

scripture

May the Lord make your love increase and overflow for each other (1 Th 3:12).

For the LORD Almighty will care for his flock (Zech 10:3).

As for God, his way is perfect (Ps 18:30).

The LORD has done great things for us, and we are filled with joy (Ps 126:3).

Children are a heritage from the LORD (Ps 127:3).

"I came that they may have life and have it abundantly" (Jn 10:10 ESV).

Personal prayer

FAITHFUL Father, we celebrate the way you have brought [child's name] into our lives. We ask for discernment as we explore all the information that could be included in her Lifebook. We ask for creativity as we write, cut, paste, arrange, and design these pieces of her history. Please show us specifically what will help give meaning to her story. Our heart's desire is that **[child's name]** will know how valuable she is as she turns each page. May she see how your fingerprints have been scattered throughout the beginning of her life. God, we know that the truth these pages contain may create feelings of confusion, fear, and rejection. Our hearts grieve for **[child's name]**'s loss, just as your heart does. May she give herself permission to grieve the pain of her relinquishment, and may she experience the peace and understanding that only you can give as she recognizes that pain and joy can and do coexist. As she reflects on each page, may you give her the eyes to see how you are putting her fragmented story back together in a hopeful and redemptive way. God, we ask for your guidance as we begin to assemble **[child's name]**'s Lifebook. We offer this sacred project to you. Amen.

Practice writing here:

PART III

Piecing It All Together

Make visible what, without you,
might never have been seen.[1]

— ROBERT BRESSON

CHAPTER 10

Visible Proof

Piecing it all together

Well, we have finally arrived at the place in this book where it all comes together. We have learned that we cannot forget, dismiss, or diminish our child's lifestory, but rather we are called to bring her story to life through the making of a Lifebook. We have learned that a Lifebook is more than a scrapbook of memories. It is a sacred story infused with the truth of our child's life prior to adoption. We have learned important lessons on timing, shaping, affirming, embracing, imagining, honoring, and prayer. We have listened to what Jesus says about our children and the importance of teaching them to listen as well. We have recognized how, through vulnerability and brokenness, the lies of the enemy can take hold of our children and distort their very identity. We have realized our children cannot "unthink" about their birth parents, just as birth parents do not want to be forgotten. Most importantly, we have seen how God's hand has shaped our families through adoption and made our hearts more like his through this amazing journey. He has placed a child in our arms to carry on the love and responsible care that he fully intended for her.

As our three children chase each other around the kitchen, laughing hysterically as they slip and slide on the hardwood floor, I watch, smile, and think, "All is well" (unless one of them falls, cracks his head, and requires stitches). I cannot imagine life without them. But, I must remember there was a time, before they were mine, when their lives existed without me.

Let's continue putting the pieces together to make visible what otherwise might not be seen.

Writing

By now, you should have one "practice writing" for each questionnaire if you have been working through the homework at the end of each chapter. These practice writings, or journalings, are probably rough, at best, at this point. Hopefully, you have freely expressed your thoughts and feelings, captured facts, events, and moments and imagined where information is missing. Hopefully these practice writings reflect your heart and you have kept it real. No one is looking, no one is judging, no one is criticizing.

Now we encourage you to do something wonderful with this information. There is so much waiting to be discovered. What stands out? Is it a special event, a moment, a reflection? Is it one word that becomes a theme? For example, in chapter 6 there are key words in the margins of the questionnaire. Choosing a key word or two can begin a free flow of thoughts. In our first sample Lifebook page, on page 152, we chose the word "born" and simply played off this theme. Rather than just reporting facts and data, we brought fullness to this page through our reflections on this child's being born. Certainly there is more to the story and you can continue to share more by creating additional pages. Perhaps on the next page you create a list from your answers to the questions or your practice writing. Our list in Sample 2 came from a medical report, which turned into a poem. Clever!

Here are some other helpful tips:

Story first

Throughout this book, we have suggested writing first. Capture the story first and let it guide your photo selection and design ideas. Looking at the overall big picture of a Lifebook, some pages will be inviting and jump out at you—the design will be part of the story. Others may have a more subdued design. For example, consider a journaling page. One mother wrote, "The pages where I talk about their (her daughters') relinquishments are plain. Just words typed on paper. Part of that is because there is a lot to say. I also feel that, of the whole story, this is the one part I can't brighten, lighten, or have fun with. I also did not want to try to cover up the hard-to-face feelings the girls will have when they do read those pages. It is sad enough and I think they should be allowed to be sad and thoughtful when they hear that part of it."

Less is more

Less is more. Using fewer photos is okay. It really is! Sometimes we feel that we have the photos and therefore we should use them all. Author and graphic designer Cathy Zielske suggests, "Grab a photo, and write down five to ten things about the person in the shot … It's quick and simple, and it tells a 'story' that's real."

Ask a question

Ask a question. Who, what, where, why, when? Ask yourself, "What am I thankful for?" "What is it about this situation, this event, this moment?" "Who is this person?" "What does this mean?" You can even answer questions your child may have. In Sample 3 we simply ask a question and answer it.

Journal

Journaling allows us to merge the facts and data with our thoughts, feelings and perceptions. We chose journaling as a way to connect with the missing people and difficult events in our child's lifestory. Samples 4 and 5 represent journaling as an idea to help share your child's story.

Choose a theme

Love, belonging, forever, memories, miracle, are just a few suggestions for a page theme. In Sample 6, we choose the theme of love. We shaped our words around our feelings of love for our child and how we became a family.

Describe

After reflecting on the answers to the questions in chapter 9, we choose to focus on the question, "What three words best describe you?" from page 141. You could choose any of these questions to craft a page. The three words that best describe our child today are bright, funny, and kind. We had fun thinking about who he is today and who he will be.

Note: If you are interested in tackling the creative work needed for a Lifebook, simply search online for a wide variety of photo book sites and scrapbooking software.

Sample Lifebook Page 1

imagine

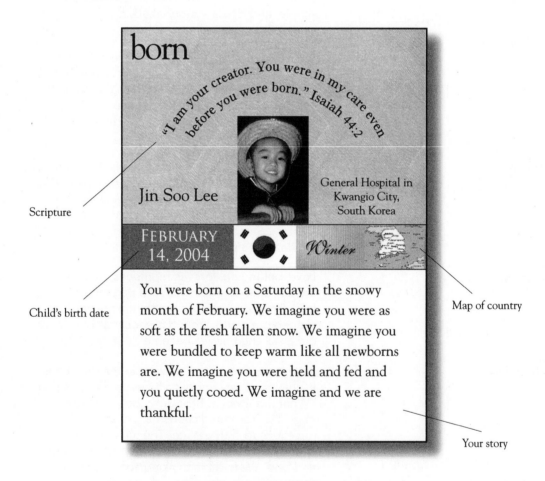

Imagine the event rather than trying to add every detail of the story to one page. Let one photo, one word, or one phrase guide you. Your child's story will spread out over more pages, but each page will have richness, depth, and focus.

Sample Lifebook Page 2

imagine

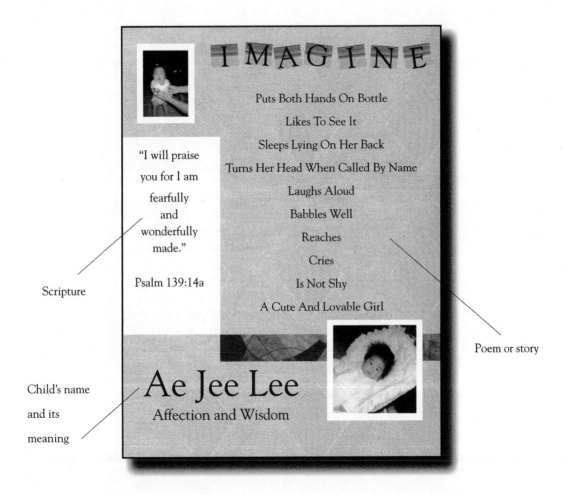

IMAGINE

Puts Both Hands On Bottle

Likes To See It

Sleeps Lying On Her Back

Turns Her Head When Called By Name

Laughs Aloud

Babbles Well

Reaches

Cries

Is Not Shy

A Cute And Lovable Girl

"I will praise you for I am fearfully and wonderfully made."

Psalm 139:14a

Ae Jee Lee
Affection and Wisdom

Scripture

Poem or story

Child's name and its meaning

Thought you did not have enough information to get started? After answering all the questions in chapter 6, you may feel as if you have too much. Overwhelmed? Use your practice writing to generate a list. Look for one topic to get started on and capture the most honest, heartfelt feelings of that topic, whether it be a photo, event, or, in this example, a medical report. Rather than simply displaying the medical report on a page, list items from the medical report. It can quickly turn into a poem.

Sample Lifebook Page 3

imagine

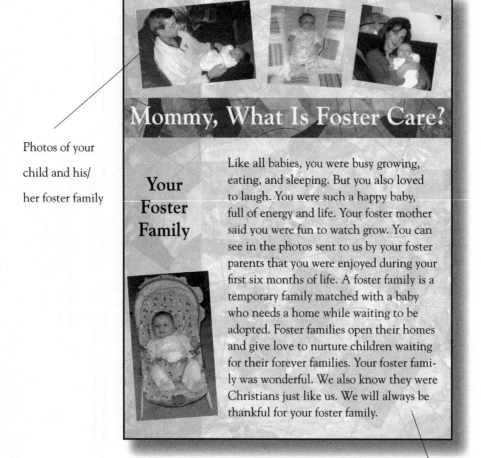

Photos of your child and his/ her foster family

Mommy, What Is Foster Care?

Your Foster Family

Like all babies, you were busy growing, eating, and sleeping. But you also loved to laugh. You were such a happy baby, full of energy and life. Your foster mother said you were fun to watch grow. You can see in the photos sent to us by your foster parents that you were enjoyed during your first six months of life. A foster family is a temporary family matched with a baby who needs a home while waiting to be adopted. Foster families open their homes and give love to nurture children waiting for their forever families. Your foster family was wonderful. We also know they were Christians just like us. We will always be thankful for your foster family.

Foster family's story

Ask a question. Our children have a lot to ask. Focus on one of their questions or ask your own. Journal to answer the question. It is that simple!

Sample Lifebook Page 4

truth

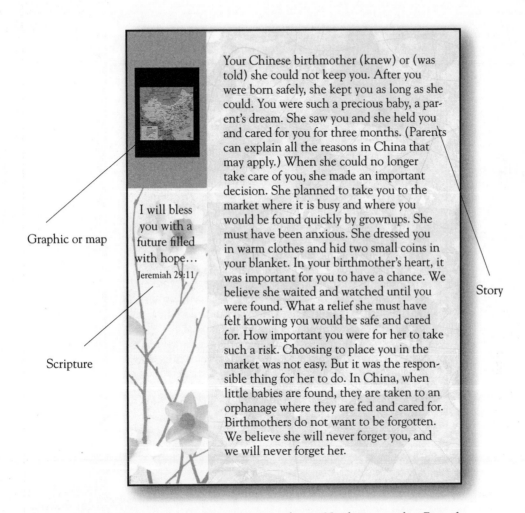

Graphic or map

I will bless you with a future filled with hope…

Jeremiah 29:11

Scripture

Your Chinese birthmother (knew) or (was told) she could not keep you. After you were born safely, she kept you as long as she could. You were such a precious baby, a parent's dream. She saw you and she held you and cared for you for three months. (Parents can explain all the reasons in China that may apply.) When she could no longer take care of you, she made an important decision. She planned to take you to the market where it is busy and where you would be found quickly by grownups. She must have been anxious. She dressed you in warm clothes and hid two small coins in your blanket. In your birthmother's heart, it was important for you to have a chance. We believe she waited and watched until you were found. What a relief she must have felt knowing you would be safe and cared for. How important you were for her to take such a risk. Choosing to place you in the market was not easy. But it was the responsible thing for her to do. In China, when little babies are found, they are taken to an orphanage where they are fed and cared for. Birthmothers do not want to be forgotten. We believe she will never forget you, and we will never forget her.

Story

As you can see, this sample page was written as a journal entry. Not fancy or perfect. First, after thoughtfully answering the questions on pages 99 and 100 in chapter 7, I sat with it all for a while and prayed. Then I began transferring my responses onto the practice writing page. I carried on as if no one was looking or would ever read it except me. This can be important in journaling because it allows thoughts to flow more freely. I imagined I would cover this page and keep it private until I knew I could safely share it. I will write a cover story too—one that will be simple enough for a young child to understand. The best thing about doing this is becoming the storyteller. Now I feel as if I know this part of the story well.

Sample Lifebook Page 5

honor

Who are my birthmother and birthfather?

Ludmilla Grigoryevna Kornok is your birthmother's name. She is from Chuvash, a region of Russia. She was born in 1965, has black hair and brown eyes and is 5'4" tall. She was almost 35 years old when she met your birthfather. He was a builder from Ukraine with black hair and brown eyes. We do not know his name. They were probably close in age. They may have dated and she became pregnant with you. Ludmilla did not marry your birthfather, but they were together for some time and eventually they no longer kept in contact. We are not sure if he knew about you. Ludmilla did not have anyone close to her to help her as she struggled to provide for herself and her five-year-old son. Living in Russia with children and without a husband is very difficult. Before you were born, your birthmother had many months to think about what she would do. She knew she could not parent you and provide what a baby needs. She had to consider your future. We believe she could not bear to put you through a life where you would struggle. Your birthmother valued life. She carried you safely and you were born healthy in the Municipal Hospital on March 17, 2000. We were told you look like your birthmother. She must have been relieved to know you were fine. It must have been hard for her to say goodbye. We see a glimpse of her heart when we see you today. We can talk about your birth parents whenever you want.

Graphic or map

Story (Parents can describe child—perhaps talents, interests, or looks that he/she received from his/her birth parents.)

Sample Lifebook Page 6a

explore

Becoming a Family

May the Lord make your love increase and overflow for each other.

(1 Tm 3:12)

We had no idea of the kind of love that comes from being a family. Was it your little toddler legs we loved to chase? Was it the way you danced to rock and roll when you were three? It was not just one thing … it was everything about you. Since we became a family, we have watched you receive love and also give it away. Our journey to you may have taken seven months, but looking back, it feels like it all happened in a blink of an eye. While we waited for you, we read books and asked lots of questions wondering how to be parents. But we realized we just had to experience it. We prayed for you, to keep you safe and healthy. We wanted to get to you fast. The highlight of our adoption story was seeing you for the first time in a snuggly onesy rubbing your face on the soft feather comforter in our hotel room in Russia. You were ours and we were yours. The low point was trying to feed you your first bottle. It didn't go well at all. Somehow we all made it. And we will always make it together because that is love and that is why we became a family.

Scripture

Story

Working through this page, I started with answering the questions found on pages 136 and 137. After that, I completed the practice writing exercise. I did not pay attention to how neatly it was written. I simply focused on writing. I then chose the word LOVE to summarize my story. Love became my guide and inspiration; I guess you would call it the glue that pieced it all together. I will write a cover story, too—one that will be simple enough for a young child to understand. The best thing about doing this is becoming the storyteller. Now I feel as if I know this part of the story well.

Sample Lifebook Page 6b

explore

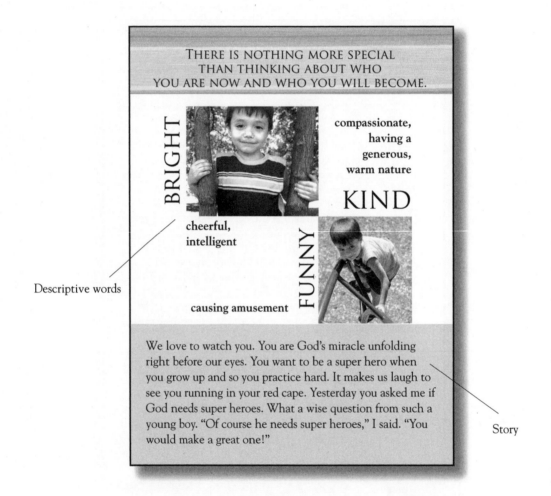

THERE IS NOTHING MORE SPECIAL
THAN THINKING ABOUT WHO
YOU ARE NOW AND WHO YOU WILL BECOME.

BRIGHT

compassionate,
having a
generous,
warm nature

KIND

cheerful,
intelligent

FUNNY

causing amusement

Descriptive words

We love to watch you. You are God's miracle unfolding right before our eyes. You want to be a super hero when you grow up and so you practice hard. It makes us laugh to see you running in your red cape. Yesterday you asked me if God needs super heroes. What a wise question from such a young boy. "Of course he needs super heroes," I said. "You would make a great one!"

Story

Look at your practice writing for chapter 9. While it may appear to be a scramble of words and thoughts, it is just what you need. Look for a key word or phrase that will help you focus. We focused on the three words we chose that best describe our child today. As you can see, a Lifebook page can offer a lot of information or just enough to get conversation going. You can continue on with more pages that capture the heart of who your child is today.

Closing paragraphs

We have never regretted the time spent on writing, designing, and creating our children's Lifebooks. We know we are making visible what otherwise might not be seen. In some ways we are taking much of the unknown out of our children's stories. We are also adding what is sacred—story, photos, documents, Scripture, and truth. And then there are the intangible messages we send to our children as they see us researching, processing, writing, designing, and presenting their stories as a precious gift crafted like none other. It will bring smiles and tears, joy and pain, concern and relief, discomfort and peace, questions and understanding. It will be shown and maybe even shunned, perhaps misunderstood, but hopefully embraced and believed.

Now that you have finished this chapter and are well on your way to piecing together each precious page, may you sense the presence of the One who has faith in you to see it through to completion. Our desire is that you will discover more of the pieces of your child's heart. May this experience bring you meaning and joy. May it bring fullness to your child's life. May it bring softness to your own heart. May it bring more of Jesus into your home.

Afterword

The other day I, Carissa, went for a ride with my dad on his motorcycle. It was sunny and warm and the breeze felt refreshing as it blew on my face. As we were getting ready to return home after stopping for a break, it began to rain. There I stood wondering, "Is this really happening?"

Everything inside of me was questioning how we could get out of having to drive forty miles home in the rain. Without hesitation, my dad invited me to "gear up," put on warm clothes, and saddle up. So, without any questions, I got on the back of the bike and we took off. As we drove through the rain, I kept thinking about the possibility of the bike tipping, how I was getting cold, and how at any moment a deer could come dashing out of the woods, causing us to get in an accident. As I sat behind my dad, I could feel my body getting tense on that little seat. And then it came to me. This is about trust. There was nothing I could do to control my surroundings. I had to trust that my dad loved me enough to protect me and drive me safely home. And so, I decided to sit back, relax, and enjoy the sacred ride home that would mysteriously bring my dad and me a little closer.

As an adult, I have come to understand how deep the impact of my relinquishment has been. I imagine myself when I was a tiny, cuddly baby—all that black hair, brown eyes, and chubby cheeks. An innocent baby so sweet and loveable. Yet, for some reason, the two people who made me chose to give me away. That hurts. My heart aches to think about what that did to my heart. I know now that, early on, I began believing the lie that I was "too much"—too much to keep, too much to love, too much to fight for. Somewhere, somehow, but for sure at a young age, I began believing that it wasn't safe to trust anyone—at least fully—and, yes, even God. What a great setup to not believe in myself and believing that I didn't have much to offer or be used by God.

But … God had a better dream.

God says that one of the ways in which he reveals his glory is through us, his creation. I was *his* creation. *He* created me, not those two people. He also says that he will make *all* things new. He has the ability to take what has been broken and put it back together again … and again and again and again. Could *this* be his heart about the amazing gift of adoption? Reveal more of himself through his beautiful and sacred creation?

Imagine with me … a little girl with squinty eyes, black hair, round face, small feet, and short stature—all the qualities that America hasn't always defined as "beautiful." She is abandoned, rejected, relinquished, and set up for failure. And then, God meets her right where she is and says, "You matter. I have come to redeem you—your past, your wounds, your pain. I see your heart, and I will mend what has been broken. You were not forgotten." And so, this little girl grows. She walks through life and experiences joy, disappointment, loss, hurt. But as she grows, she realizes that it is both in her joy *and* pain that she is joined with God. She hears him gently whisper, "You can trust me."

So now she has a choice. She could abandon her Creator just as she was abandoned, or she could choose to reclaim her broken past and use it for good. She could live in despair and hopelessness, or she could allow the impact of her relinquishment to be used for her own transformation and to bring glory to God. Maybe it's not about forgetting the past, but embracing it—reclaiming it—using it for good and allowing God to reveal himself *through* it.

It is *then* when you can sit back, enjoy the ride, and actually feel the refreshing breeze on your face. It is *then* when you can experience true, deep, authentic intimacy with God.

See, it's about trust.

God is putting me back together over and over again, and I am invited to be a part of *that* story.

A Small Group
Experience

Sharing personal stories, learning and understanding new concepts, processing different viewpoints, being inspired to put new ideas into action—this is just the beginning of how a small group could utilize *Before You Were Mine*. This book was designed to benefit individuals, families, and small group ministries. Imagine a safe environment where group members receive support, encouragement, wisdom, and inspiration through meaningful discussions and shared experience—a place where you could learn how to bring fullness to your adopted child's story.

In Part I of *Before You Were Mine* helpful questions appear at the end of each chapter. These help stimulate authentic, face-to-face conversations. These questions will stir up stories of the joys, challenges, fears, questions, and thoughts that many adoptive parents encounter.

Part II of the book provides specific exercises in the form of questionnaires. These are designed to capture the intimate details of your child's beginning and to help prepare you for the writing experience. In a group setting, such as in a church or community small group, the research and findings can lead to additional Lifebook material, creative ideas, shared resources, and more conversations that will make everyone's Lifebook fuller and richer. In the end, the group will be able to put desire into action as, together, the pieces of your child's lifestory will unfold into a meaningful and creative Lifebook.

Your adopted child's birth history is more than a fading memory. It is a sacred story waiting to be revealed. Consider starting a ministry for adoptive families by offering a small group experience using *Before You Were Mine* as a guide.

Resources

Books

These books may be helpful in making your child's Lifebook:

Telling the Truth to Your Adopted or Foster Child: Making Sense of the Past, by Betsy Keefer and Jayne E. Schooler

Twenty Things Adopted Kids Wish Their Adoptive Parents Knew, by Sherrie Eldridge

Parenting the Hurt Child, by Gregory C. Keck and Regina M. Kupecky

Toddler Adoption: The Weaver's Craft, by Mary Hopkins Best

Power of a Praying Parent, by Stormie Omartian

The Five Love Languages of Children, by Gary Chapman, PH.D. and Ross Cambell

Too Busy Not to Pray, by Bill Hybels with LaVonne Neff

Leading Your Child to Jesus, by David Staal

I Wish for You a Beautiful Life: Letters from the Korean Birthmothers of AE Ran Won to Their Children, edited by Sara Dorow

Does Anybody Else Look Like Me? A Parent's Guide to Raising Multiracial Children, by Donna Jackson Nakazawa

Beneath the Mask: Understanding Adopted Teens, by Debbie Riley, M.S., with John Meeks, M.D.

Parenting Teens with Love and Logic, by Foster Cline, M.D., and Jim Fay

Notes

Foreword

1. Ezell, Lee, *The Missing Piece* (Ventura, CA: Regal Books, 2004).

Introduction

1. O'Malley, Beth, *Lifebooks: Creating A Treasure for the Adopted Child* (Winthrop, MA: Adoption Works, 2002).

Overview

1. O'Malley, Beth, op. cit.
2. Ibid., 7.

Chapter 1

1. Probst, Cindy, *Adoption Lifebook: A Bridge To Your Child's Beginnings: A Workbook for International Adoptive Families* (Boston: Boston Adoption Press, 2002), 13.
2. Keefer, Betsy, and Jayne E. Schooler, *Telling the Truth to Your Adopted or Foster Child, Making Sense of the Past* (Westport, CT; London: Bergin & Garvey, 2000), 14.
3. Nydam, Ronald J., *Adoptees Come of Age* (Louisville, KY: Westminster John Knox Press, 1999), 14.
4. Sharma, Anu, and Debbie Riley, "Special Report, Adoption & Teens, Part I: The Psychological Background: Reprint of Nagging Questions," *Adoptive Families Magazine* (July/August 1996).
5. Eldridge, Sherrie, *Twenty Things Adopted Kids Wish Their Adoptive Parents Knew* (New York: Dell Publishing, 1999), 12.
6. Keefer and Schooler, op.cit., 29.

Chapter 2

1. Burns, John, *The Miracle in a Daddy's Hug* (New York: Howard Books, 2003), 39.
2. ten Boom, Corrie, from www.thinkexist.com.
3. Kopp, Harpham Heather, *Praying the Bible for Your Baby*, (Colorado Springs: Waterbrook Press, 1998), 2.
4. Warren, Rick, *The Purpose Driven Life* (Grand Rapids: Zondervan, 2002), 23.
5. Keefer and Schooler, op.cit., 22.
6. MacInnes, Carolyn, "Life Books" at TroubledWith: a website of Focus on the Family, www.troubledwith.com, 2004.
7. Trent, John; Rick Osborne; and Kurt Bruner, eds. *Parents' Guide to the Spiritual Growth of Children, Helping Your Child Develop a Personal Faith* (Wheaton, IL: Tyndale House, 2000).
8. Ibid., 232.
9. Weidmann, Jim, and Marianne Hering, *The Power of Teachable Moments: Using Everyday Experiences to Teach Your Child about God* (Wheaton, IL: Tyndale House, 2004), 37.

Chapter 3

1. McClain, Lee ToBin, Ph.D., "Telling the Tough Stuff," *Adoptive Families Magazine* (September/October 2005), 34–37.
2. Fahlberg, Vera, "The Life Story Book," Pact, An Adoption Alliance (1998), www.pactadopt.org.
3. Keefer and Schooler, op.cit., 54.
4. Fahlberg, Vera, op.cit.
5. Reisser, Paul C., M.D., *The Complete Book of Baby and Child Care*, Focus on the Family (Wheaton, IL: Tyndale House, 1997), 411.
6. O'Malley, Beth, op. cit., 19.
7. MacInnes, Carolyn, op. cit.
8. Trent, John; Rick Osborne; and Kurt Bruner, op. cit., 135.
9. Nakazawa, Donna Jackson, *Does Anybody Else Look Like Me? A Parent's Guide to Raising Multiracial Children* (Cambridge, MA: Perseus Publishing, 2003) 138.
10. Probst, Cindy, op. cit., 45.
11. Keefer and Schooler, op.cit., 17.
12. Fahlberg, Vera, op.cit.

Chapter 4

1. Kopp, Heather Harpham, *Praying the Bible for Your Baby* (Colorado Springs: Waterbrook Press, 1998), 2.
2. Omartian, Stormie, *The Power of a Praying Parent* (Eugene, OR: Harvest House, 1995), 20.
3. Nouwen, Henri: quote taken from *A More Excellent Way: A Journal of Personal Growth*, compiled by Dr. Terry Wardle (Ashland, OH: Sandberg Leadership Center of Ashland Theological Seminary).
4. Guthrie, Nancy, "Prayers That Move the Heart of God," *Today's Christian Woman* (March/April 2006), 22–24.

Chapter 6

1. *The Complete Book of Baby and Child Care*, op. cit., 113–539.
2. Nakazawa, Donna Jackson, Phone interview: Discussion on racial identity and adoption (October 19, 2006).
3. Rohr, Richard: quote taken from *A More Excellent Way: A Journal of Personal Growth*, op. cit.

Chapter 7

1. Moore, Beth, *Believing God* (Nashville: Broadman & Holman, 2004), 92.
2. Bronson, Megan, "Grief & Loss and Growth Counseling" (Belmont, MI: Balance Point, Inc.), email, summer 2006.
3. Keefer and Schooler, op.cit., 195.
4. Eldridge, Sherrie, op. cit., p. 73.
5. Adesman, Andrew, M.D., with Christine Adamec, *Parenting Your Adopted Child: A Positive Approach to Building a Strong Family* (New York: McGraw–Hill, 2004), 143.
6. Keefer and Schooler, op. cit., 92.
7. Adesman, Andrew, M.D., with Christine Adamec, op. cit., 141.

Chapter 8

1. Barber, Margaret Fairless, WorldofQuotes.com.
2. Eldridge, Sherrie, email, December 2005.

3. Miller, Kathryn Anne, and Jami Moffett, *Did My First Mother Love Me? A Story for an Adopted Child* (Buena Park, CA: Morning Glory Press, 1994).

4. Evans, Karin, *The Lost Daughters of China* (New York: Tarcher, 2001), 83–84.

5. Eldridge, Sherrie, personal email, November 6, 2006.

6. Wolf, Jana, "Paradoxes of Adoptive Parenting," *Adoptive Families Magazine* (March/April 2006), 42.

7. Miller, Kathryn Anne, and Jami Moffett, op. cit., 45.

8. Nydam, Ronald J., op. cit., 56.

9. Klein, Jenny, LBSW, birth parent counselor (Holland, MI: Bethany Christian Services), email, November 2006.

10. Keck, Gregory, C., email, July 2005.

Chapter 9

1. Whalen, Jeanne, "Russia's Healthcare Is Crumbling," *The Wall Street Journal* (February 13, 2004), A9, A10.

2. Nesler, Joey, "Questions about Birth Siblings," *Adoptive Families Magazine* (July/August 2006), 49.

Chapter 10

1. Bresson, Robert, *Notes on the Cinematographer* (Los Angeles: Green Integer, May 1997).

2. Warren, Rick, op. cit., 261.

Scripture Versions

The following Scripture versions are quoted in this book in addition to the New International Version.

Scripture quotations marked NKJV are taken from the New King James Version. Copyright © 1982, by Thomas Nelson, Inc. Used by permission. All rights reserved.

Scripture quotations marked NCV are taken from the *Holy Bible, New Century Version*. Copyright © 1987, 1988, 1991. Used by permission of Word Publishing.

Scripture quotations marked NLV are taken from the Holy Bible, New Life Version, copyright © 1969–2003, Christian Life International, P.O. Box 777, Canby, OR 97013. Used by permission.

Scripture quotations marked TLB or The Living Bible are taken from *The Living Bible* © 1971 by Tyndale House Publishers, Inc., Wheaton, Illinois. All rights reserved.

Scripture quotations marked TEV are taken from *Today's English Version*. © American Bible Society 1966, 1971, 1976, 1992.

Scripture quotations marked CEV are taken from *The Contemporary English Version: with Apocrypha*. © 1995 by the American Bible Society. Used by permission.

Scripture quotations marked ESV are taken from *The Holy Bible: English Standard Version*, copyright © 2001, by Crossway Bibles, a division of Good News Publishers. Used by permission. All rights reserved.

Scripture quotations marked MSG are taken from *THE MESSAGE*. Copyright © 1993, 1994, 1995, 1996, 2000, 2001, 2002. Used by permission of NavPress Publishing Group.

Acknowledgments

Writing a book is all about making it happen in the midst of life. As much as our lives were shaped for writing (and while writing) this book, many others took time out of their lives to help. We thank all those who contributed their stories for the pages of this book. We are deeply grateful for your willingness to be honest and vulnerable about your adoption experiences.

From Susan...

A special thank you to several extraordinary moms: Jill DeJong, Lori Melton, Laurel Shippert, Denise Edgecomb, and Merri Jo Fey—for long talks and soul bearing. To Cindy Walter—my first Lifebook accountability partner. To Sherrie Eldridge, adoption advocate and author, I treasure our friendship and your tender support over the years through emails and phone calls—thank you for encouraging me. For this chance of a lifetime to impact the adoption community, I especially thank our extraordinary managing editor, Jim Ruark at Zondervan. To our dear friends, Kathy and Chad Williams—great book title! To my husband Mike and our incredible children, Matthew, Kola, and Lera—thank you for sharing me and your stories.

From Carissa...

Writing this book has been an unexpected part of my story—one that has taken me to the deeper places of my heart, which has invited me to receive more of God's healing and love and delight. So, Susan, thank you for inviting me to go here with you. For believing in the message of our book, I thank all those at Zondervan who had a part in getting our book "on the shelf." For the incredible words of wisdom and insight, I thank my wonderful father and Matt Krick. For the long talks, friendship, and perspective of the amazing gift of motherhood, I thank all my mom friends. For the pure joy and excitement about this book, I thank Susie Hayes. For teaching me that the story of my heart matters, I thank Kathryn Christensen. For the consistent encouragement and love and belief in me as a person, I thank my husband, Matt. For all the moments that are filled with awe and wonder and beauty, I thank my children, Skyla and Zane.

About the Authors

Susan A. TeBos is the mother of three internationally adopted children. She is actively involved in her local adoption community, presenting to groups, advocating for respite resources, and coming alongside other adoptive families needing support. Susan holds a master's degree in communication from Western Michigan University. She lives with her husband and children in Grand Rapids, Michigan.

Carissa R. Woodwyk is a Korean adoptee. She holds a master's degree in counseling psychology and is a licensed counselor and marriage and family therapist. She enjoys speaking on relationships, marriage, personal growth, identity, and adoption. She and her husband have two children and live in Hudsonville, Michigan.

Practice writing here:

Practice writing here:

Practice writing here:

Practice writing here:

Practice writing here:

Practice writing here:

Share Your Thoughts

With the Author: Your comments will be forwarded to the author when you send them to *zauthor@zondervan.com*.

With Zondervan: Submit your review of this book by writing to *zreview@zondervan.com*.

Free Online Resources at
www.zondervan.com

Zondervan AuthorTracker: Be notified whenever your favorite authors publish new books, go on tour, or post an update about what's happening in their lives at www.zondervan.com/authortracker.

Daily Bible Verses and Devotions: Enrich your life with daily Bible verses or devotions that help you start every morning focused on God. Visit www.zondervan.com/newsletters.

Free Email Publications: Sign up for newsletters on Christian living, academic resources, church ministry, fiction, children's resources, and more. Visit www.zondervan.com/newsletters.

Zondervan Bible Search: Find and compare Bible passages in a variety of translations at www.zondervanbiblesearch.com.

Other Benefits: Register to receive online benefits like coupons and special offers, or to participate in research.

ZONDERVAN®

ZONDERVAN.com/
AUTHORTRACKER
follow your favorite authors